GAZING

AT

GOD

Books by Sharon Hodde Miller

Free of Me
Nice
The Cost of Control
Gazing at God

GAZING

AT

GOD

A 40-Day Journey to Greater Freedom from Self

SHARON HODDE MILLER

BakerBooks

a division of Baker Publishing Group
Grand Rapids, Michigan

Published by Baker Books
a division of Baker Publishing Group
Grand Rapids, Michigan
BakerBooks.com

Printed in the United States of America

Library of Congress Cataloging-in-Publication Data
Names: Miller, Sharon Hodde, 1981– author.
Title: Gazing at God : a 40-day journey to greater freedom from self / Sharon
    Hodde Miller.
Description: Grand Rapids, Michigan : Baker Books, a division of Baker Publishing
    Group, [2025] | Includes bibliographical references.
Identifiers: LCCN 2024035367 | ISBN 9781540904232 (cloth) | ISBN
    9781493450381 (ebook)
Subjects: LCSH: Faith. | Trust in God. | Devotional calendars.
Classification: LCC BT771.3 .M56 2025 | DDC 242/.2—dc23/eng/20241026
LC record available at https://lccn.loc.gov/2024035367

Cover design by Lindy Kasler.

Published in association with The Bindery Agency, www.TheBinderyAgency.com.

Baker Publishing Group publications use paper produced from sustainable forestry practices and postconsumer waste whenever possible.

25 26 27 28 29 30 31   7 6 5 4 3 2 1

For Jesus.
Because these pages contain insights
from the second-greatest liberation of my life—
second only to finding you.

CONTENTS

Contents

Movement 4 • Turning toward God

Movement 5 • Turning toward Others

BEFORE YOU BEGIN

In 2017 I released my first book, *Free of Me*, in which I documented my struggle with self-preoccupation. At the time of its release, I remember feeling both excited about how it might encourage people and terrified that no one would relate. On the one hand, the lessons in that book had provided me the single greatest freedom of my life, second only to meeting Jesus—a freedom I continue to walk in today—and I was certain others would experience the same. On the other hand, I wondered if my self-focus was somewhat unique to me. I wondered if people would read my story and brush it off as my own sick narcissism. "This sounds like a *you* problem," I could already hear people saying, disgusted by my vanity.

Thankfully, that is not at all what happened. Instead, the message resonated far and wide. I heard from women in college, women in their eighties, men pastoring churches, and individuals from all over the world who related to this struggle. Years later, I still hear from readers on a weekly basis.

As it turns out, I was not unique.

That said, I have continued to learn more about self-forgetfulness and its freedoms. Since *Free of Me*'s release, I have planted a church with my husband, had another child, and written more books, all the while walking out the message of freedom from self. Along the way, I have experienced new levels of freedom and reached new layers of understanding, and because of this, I have long felt that I had more to say.

Which leads to the purpose of this devotional.

About midway through *Free of Me* I tell a story about my mom's antique Steinway piano. The instrument was meticulously crafted more than one hundred years ago and is paneled with dark, polished mahogany and a satin finish. It is the most beautiful piano I have ever seen, and it is a literal masterpiece, but it still needs regular tuning. Despite the high quality of the instrument, the quality of its *sound* is not fixed. Instead, this piano naturally drifts out of tune. This is true of most instruments: no matter the excellence of the material, no matter the expertise of the craftsman, an instrument's sound will eventually *bend* off course and out of tune.

I liken that Steinway to the human soul, which also has a tendency to drift. We are made by the finest Craftsman in the universe, but our souls nevertheless bend and warp. This is exactly the way the ancient theologian St. Augustine describes the effects of sin. Sin causes the soul to *bend in on itself*. We, like a musical instrument, need constant unbending. We regularly need to retune ourselves to the gospel of Jesus.

That is the purpose of this devotional. If you feel pain or insecurity as a result of your soul being turned inward, I hope this forty-day devotional will be a helpful guide in reorienting yourself back toward God and others. To raising your gaze.

At the same time, let me be clear about something. For Augustine, what "unbends the soul" is not reading the Bible, spending a lot of time in prayer, or participating in countless religious activities. In short, it's not works. What draws our souls outward and reorients us toward the love of God and neighbor is not effort, but grace. While we do have a role to play in our own spiritual healing, the freedom we are ultimately after is not something we can earn. This devotional is a tool, but it is God who gives the growth.

Defining the Terms

Before you embark on this journey, there are a couple terms that I would like to define, and the first is deceptively basic: the **self**. We hold no worldly possession closer than the self, yet it is surprisingly difficult to pin down, because there can be a chasm between our true selves and our perception of ourselves. That is why I like psychologist Dr. Alison Cook's framing of "selfhood" in her book *The Best of You*. In it she writes, "*Selfhood* is a psychological term that refers to your individual identity—your 'you-ness.' . . . It's what makes you a distinct person from everyone around you."[1] This definition points to the reality that the self is an objective, unique identity, dreamed up and handed to us by God. Our sense of self is complicated and evolving and sometimes downright wrong, but that does not change the truth or distinctness of our individual identities.

The second term I would like to define is **self-forgetfulness**, a less familiar concept for many of us. To begin, what self-forgetfulness does *not* mean is ignoring the self or repressing the self. Nor does it mean the self is bad. Instead, self-forgetfulness refers to a kind of freedom, freedom from being distracted by or preoccupied with the self, so that we are then free to love God and others. As theologian Tim Keller put it in his book *The Freedom of Self-Forgetfulness*, "The essence of gospel-humility is not thinking more of myself or thinking less of myself, it is thinking of myself less."[2]

The Five Movements of Self-Forgetfulness

This book is structured around five different stages in the journey to self-forgetfulness; however, this progression is not so much a line with an endpoint as it is a cycle that we journey through, over and over again.

Movement 1: Noticing Your Self

We cannot forget the self until we first understand the self. This stage invites us to examine ourselves without judgment or shame so that we can assess our habits of thought, our sin patterns, our motivations, and perhaps most importantly, our pain.

Movement 2: Receiving Your True Self

Self-denial must not be confused with self-rejection or a denigration of the self. This stage, therefore, establishes the goodness of the self, biblically and theologically, and what it means to receive our "true self."

Movement 3: Denying the Self

While self-denial is, in many ways, an active practice, it is also an opportunity we receive. This section focuses primarily on reframing our moments of humiliation and insecurity as invitations to greater freedom in Christ.

Movement 4: Turning toward God

We experience greater freedom from the self as we raise our gaze onto our true source of joy, security, peace, and belonging. As we focus on God, it draws us out of the crushing smallness of self-preoccupation.

Movement 5: Turning toward Others

The two greatest commandments are to love God and love our neighbor, and both practices "unbend" our souls in liberating ways. In this final section, we learn how to "consider others as more important than [ourselves]" (Phil. 2:3) out of love for them but also for the sake of healing our own vision.

How to Use This Devotional

Each day of this devotional can be read on its own, meaning you can read it in order or you can pick up this devotional, flip to the middle, and go. You can also read through it at your own pace. My simple prayer is that this devotional will give you new language and tools to turn your insecurities into places of freedom.

With all of that in mind, I invite you now to pause and ask God for that kind of freedom. Ask him to accomplish in you that which you cannot accomplish on your own. And ask him to help you see that which you cannot see on your own.

I pray, as I write this, that you will find him faithful in this journey.

Movement 1

———

NOTICING
YOUR
SELF

Notice Yourself

Without knowledge of self, there is no knowledge of God.

JOHN CALVIN

Then the man and his wife heard the sound of the LORD God as he was walking in the garden in the cool of the day, and they hid from the LORD God among the trees of the garden. But the LORD God called to the man, "Where are you?"

Genesis 3:8–9 NIV

The journey to self-forgetfulness begins with a paradox: We forget the self by first examining the self. Strange, isn't it?

But necessary. We cannot simply resolve to focus on God or be more considerate of others. We cannot simply make up our minds to fixate on ourselves less. We need to understand *why* we are centering ourselves in the first place. What's behind our self-preoccupation? What is going on inside of our hearts and our minds? Is it simply pride, or could it be pain? Until we can answer those questions accurately, we will be treating the symptoms rather than the source. That is why these first few days will be spent *noticing*, pausing long enough to search the self and, more importantly, to let God search us.

Part of the reason we should start here is that this is where God starts with Adam immediately after the fall. In the aftermath of Adam and Eve's first act of defiance and self-reliance (Gen. 3), God asks Adam this simple question: "Where are you?"

What an odd question for the Creator of the universe to ask. Had God really been baffled by Adam's hiding place? Of course, the answer is no. God is omniscient, which means this question is rhetorical. God is not searching for Adam but inviting Adam to search himself. He is giving Adam the opportunity to pause and ask, "How did I get here? Why did I listen to a talking snake? Why didn't I ask any questions? Why did I doubt God's goodness so easily?"

Unfortunately, Adam is unable to do any of this internal work. Instead, he simply raises his finger and blames Eve.

This is Adam's second tragic mistake. Had he stopped long enough to examine himself, to notice what was really going on in his own soul, he might have experienced true healing and comfort.

Instead, he blames.

Too often, we make the same mistake. We don't take the time—or *make* the time—to sit with ourselves and consider the real reason we are fragile and insecure. Instead, we jump immediately to blame. "I feel insecure because . . ."

"They didn't invite me."

"They didn't acknowledge me."

"They rejected me."

"They judged me."

"I was never good enough for them."

"He never liked me."

"She always made comments about my body."

These are, without a doubt, deeply painful experiences. Jesus endured many of these wounds himself. However, these are only the surface reasons for our struggles with insecurity. There is, in fact, another layer—a *deeper* layer to our insecurities—but to discover it, we need to move beyond what happened *to* us and instead examine what is going on *inside of* us.

Rather than blame, we might consider asking questions like . . .

"Am I insecure because my identity is built on the foundation of something insecure?"

"Does my self-esteem fluctuate because it is dependent on my performance?"

"Is my need for belonging insatiable?"

"Am I looking for others to heal something inside me that only God can heal?"

Or perhaps the question we need to ask ourselves is less specific. Perhaps we need to step back and ask the same question God initially posed to Adam: "Right now, where am I? What is going on inside my heart?"

Too often we get so distracted by the people and situations that trigger our insecurities that we never consider what our insecurities are telling us about our souls. This initial stage—the noticing stage, the observing stage, the discovering stage—is where we need to start. We need to begin by considering what information our insecurities provide. What idols do they reveal? What patterns? What unhealed wounds?

These are the first questions we need to answer, as honestly as we can, without an ounce of condemnation or shame and with the help of the Holy Spirit.

REFLECT: Where are you? Right now—in this week or in this season—what is going on in your heart and mind? Do you notice any insecurities, and if so, what might be underneath them?

Notice Your Scripts

We become the stories we tell ourselves.
MICHAEL CUNNINGHAM

Suddenly, the word of the Lord came to him, and [God]
said to him, "What are you doing here, Elijah?"

He replied, "I have been very zealous for the LORD
God of Armies, but the Israelites have abandoned
your covenant, torn down your altars, and killed your
prophets with the sword. I alone am left, and they are
looking for me to take my life."

1 Kings 19:9–10

In 1 Kings 19, the prophet Elijah does something extremely relatable.

Discouraged, burned-out, and fearful for his life, he collapses in the presence of God and unloads. In verse 4 he declares, "I have had enough! LORD, take my life." In verse 10 he elaborates on his despair, essentially saying, "I have worked so hard for you, but no one has listened to me. Your people have rejected you, and your prophets, and I'm the only one left."

Elijah's despair in this moment is understandable. Jezebel, the notorious wife of King Ahab, has slaughtered many of the Lord's prophets, and now she is coming for him. Anyone in his position would be terrified.

However, fear is not the only emotion Elijah is experiencing in this moment. In addition to panic and despair, there is also self-pity.

Notice, for instance, how quickly Elijah gives up. He has been in public ministry for only three years, and during that time he has participated in miracle after miracle. He raised a woman's son from the dead. He humiliated the prophets of Baal and oversaw their execution. When he was hungry, God sent ravens to feed him. *Ravens.* By any measure, Elijah is extraordinarily favored by God. He succeeds in all that he does, in the most dazzling displays of spiritual power imaginable. Everything he touches turns to gold.

Until it doesn't, and then we see a very different side of Elijah. At the first major obstacle in his ministry, Elijah collapses into despair. He wants to give up, and he even wants to die. This is the first clue that Elijah's vision is beginning to warp.

But it doesn't stop there. He makes the unsubstantiated claim that *all* of God's people have turned away and that he is the *only* prophet left. This, too, is not reality. In

1 Kings 18:13—just one chapter earlier—Obadiah tells Elijah that one hundred other prophets have been spared, which means Elijah *knows* he is not the only prophet left. Elijah *knows* he is not alone.

In other words, these sweeping statements about his superiority and isolation are not factual statements but emotional ones. In his fatigue, Elijah is rewriting the story, and one sign that he is doing this is the many "I" statements he uses in chapter 19:

> "*I* have had enough! Lord, take my life" (v. 4).
>
> "*I'm* no better than my ancestors" (v. 4).
>
> "*I* have been very zealous for the Lord God of Armies, but the Israelites have abandoned your covenant" (v. 10).
>
> "*I* alone am left" (v. 10).

Elijah is a prophet of the Lord, but the primary story he is telling is a story about himself. In his version, he is the protagonist. He is the center. And this tells us a lot about what is going on in his interior world. Studies show that this sort of me-centered language, in which a person constantly references themselves, is an indicator of depression and other mental illness.[1] Whenever we find ourselves spiraling into narratives featuring "I, I, I" or "me, me, me" language, we can take that as a good indicator that something inside of us is unwell.

That said, this me-centered language is not simply a "check engine light." Self-centered scripts fuel our insecurities as well. When we are at the center of our own stories—"What do they think of *me*? Why didn't they include *me*? Why doesn't anyone appreciate *me*?"—we begin to lose perspective, not because thinking about ourselves is inherently wrong or misguided but because it stops us from being able to see anything else.

That is exactly what happens to Elijah. His self-focus becomes his entire focus. He cannot see God's faithfulness in the past, nor does he remember the other remaining prophets. Instead, he narrates a distorted version of reality because he is using himself—and how he is feeling at the moment—as his primary lens.

Elijah's story is thus a cautionary tale, challenging us to pay attention to our own scripts. Whenever we process our experiences of insecurity or pain, we would be wise to notice how much of our story is centered on ourselves. We can ask, "How much of the story is about *me*? How they didn't consider *me*? How they didn't apologize to *me*?"

Perhaps that script is an important indicator that there is something else going on underneath.

REFLECT: Can you name any recurring scripts in your life? When your insecurity is triggered, what are some of the common ways you narrate the reasons for it?

Notice Your Assumptions

Assumptions are dangerous things to make, and like all dangerous things to make—bombs, for instance, or strawberry shortcake—if you make even the tiniest mistake you can find yourself in terrible trouble.

LEMONY SNICKET

There was a famine in the land, so Abram went down to Egypt to stay there for a while because the famine in the land was severe. When he was about to enter Egypt, he said to his wife, Sarai, "Look, I know what a beautiful woman you are. When the Egyptians see you, they will say, 'This is his wife.' They will kill me but let you live. Please say you're my sister so it will go well for me because of you, and my life will be spared on your account."

Genesis 12:10–13

A uthor and researcher Brené Brown once wrote that "clear is kind."[1] By this, she meant that one of the simplest ways we can express care for one another is by eliminating confusion, ambiguity, or gaps in information in our communication.

Why is this kind?

Because in the absence of information, humans are terribly quick to assume.

Consider for a moment the last time you miscommunicated with a coworker, a family member, or a friend. Perhaps it was the wording of their text message, the tone of their voice, or that they didn't call you back. Whenever you are faced with this kind of ambiguity, you might rush to make sense of it. Rather than wait for the dust to settle, for the facts to emerge, or for the chance to ask someone directly, you try to connect the dots yourself. And interestingly, you almost always do this using the filter of *self*:

"He is in a bad mood because of something *I* did."

"She didn't call me back because she is angry with *me*."

"She flew off the handle because of *my* behavior."

"He ghosted me after several dates because something is wrong with *me*."

Each of these examples demonstrates the essential nature of assumptions, whose gravitational pull is usually selfward. Whenever we are faced with a lack of clarity, we tend to fill in every gap, every bit of missing information, with an invented story in which we are the central character.

And, unfortunately, the story we write is usually negative.

Take Abram, for example. In Genesis 12, God commissions him into a special calling, but God is vague about the details. Notice there is a clear vision but no plan:

> The LORD said to Abram:
>
>> Go from your land,
>> your relatives,
>> and your father's house
>> to the land that I will show you.
>> I will make you into a great nation,
>> I will bless you,
>> I will make your name great,
>> and you will be a blessing.
>> I will bless those who bless you,
>> I will curse anyone who treats you with contempt,
>> and all the peoples on earth
>> will be blessed through you. (vv. 1–3)

Despite the fact that God is being exceptionally generous with Abram, he is also casting a high-level vision with no on-the-ground directions. God does not explain where exactly he is calling Abram. Nor does he explain why he chose Abram in the first place. There is very little in the way of concrete details. It's all lofty and visionary, and so, in the absence of those details, Abram fills in the gaps . . .

with himself. Abram assumes he is the center of the story and makes decisions accordingly.

He uses this self-centered filter when he enters Egypt. Abram immediately assumes all eyes will be on him (and his wife), which is why he takes active steps to protect himself, by passing off Sarai as his sister.

This is where our me-centered scripts lead us: to make assumptions that depart from reality. Whenever we notice these scripts playing out in our heads, it's helpful to pause and consider what *assumptions* are sneaking in with them:

> "Is he in a bad mood because of me, or is it because there is something else happening in his life that I don't know about?"
>
> "Did she fail to call me back because she is angry with me, or is it because she has a full-time job and kids, or perhaps she is caring for an aging parent?"
>
> "Did she lose her temper because of me, or is it because she has an issue with control?"
>
> "Did he ghost me because of some personality defect in myself, or is he simply unthoughtful?"

Whenever we find ourselves in relational ambiguity, we must resist the urge to make assumptions. More than that, we must resist the urge to assume that their behavior is about *us*. Even if, in the end, a person's behavior *is* about us, it is not our responsibility to sleuth that out. Whenever we try to read other people's minds, we will not only draw false conclusions about them but also do a lot of damage in the process. To others and to ourselves.

REFLECT: Consider the last time you felt anxious or insecure in relational ambiguity. What sorts of assumptions were fueling those feelings?

Notice Your Pain

My heart shudders within me;
terrors of death sweep over me.
Fear and trembling grip me;
horror has overwhelmed me.
I said, "If only I had wings like a dove!
I would fly away and find rest.
How far away I would flee;
I would stay in the wilderness. *Selah*
I would hurry to my shelter
from the raging wind and the storm." . . .

Now it is not an enemy who insults me—
otherwise I could bear it;
it is not a foe who rises up against me—
otherwise I could hide from him.
But it is you, a man who is my peer,
my companion and good friend!

Psalm 55:4–8, 12–13

I was giving my ten-month-old son a bath one night when I noticed a sharp pain in my side. *That's strange*, I thought, but I quickly chalked it up to indigestion. As the evening went on, however, the pain returned in waves and steadily increased. My husband was out of town, so I tried to stay calm, but in addition to the pain I also felt very confused by the way it was manifesting. Why did I feel like I was in labor?

As the pain continued to escalate, I practiced the breathing techniques I had used while giving birth, but they did not help at all. Eventually, I was writhing on the floor on the verge of tears, still unsure of what to do. I finally thought to text a neighbor who rushed over to my house, and as soon as she saw me on the floor, she called 911.

By the end of the night, I was admitted to a nearby hospital where I was given a battery of tests, and eventually I had an answer to this strange, stabbing pain: I was having a gallbladder attack. Apparently gallbladders can attack!

Many years have passed since I rolled around on the floor that day. There are a lot of details I do not remember—such as the length of the ambulance ride or how I passed the hours while waiting in the emergency department—but no matter how much time goes by, I can tell you with absolute certainty what I was NOT thinking about:

I was not thinking about the emails I needed to respond to.

I was not thinking about the errands I needed to run.

I was not thinking about the homework I had to finish
(I was in graduate school at the time).
I was not even thinking about my son's bedtime.

I wasn't thinking about any of those logistical details.
But I wasn't thinking about bigger, nobler concerns either.
My life didn't flash before my eyes. I didn't wonder about
my purpose on earth or the future of my family. I did not
suddenly receive a vision for world peace.

There was only one thing I was thinking about and that
was the pain. It eclipsed everything else. I was solely and
completely concentrated on how to endure it and how to
alleviate it.

That is the essential nature of pain. Its vision is inward
and small, which is necessary for immediate survival. If you
fracture your foot, the immediate priority is taking care of
that foot. And until your foot heals, you are going to pay
it a lot of attention. In order to accommodate that injury,
you may change your schedule, your activities, even the
way you walk.

That is what pain does. It has a way of stealing the spot-
light, which is actually a good thing. Pain is your body's way
of asking for the care and attention it needs, and emotional
pain is the same. Sometimes our focus is small and selfward
because we are in *pain*. Our self-focus is a sign that the self
is suffering.

Pain is an important exception when we are talking
about self-forgetfulness, because self-focus is not always
about vanity or pride. Sometimes self-focus is a sign that

some part of our self is wounded and in need of care, which means we cannot be free of self-focus until we attend to the pain that is causing it.

This is the gracious invitation of Psalm 55 and other psalms of lament. In these poems, David goes into astonishing detail about his pain, examining his wounds from every conceivable angle. In Psalm 22, for example, he writes graphic descriptions of the anguish he is experiencing, almost like a catalog of injuries: bones out of joint, a heart melted like wax, a tongue so dry it sticks to the roof of his mouth. These are not meant to be taken literally but are instead depictions of psychological agony.

We don't always associate the Psalms with this sort of grief and angst. They are more often celebrated for their poetic expressions of worship, not the stormy landscape of David's interior world. But the Psalms contain a good bit of both. The glory of God, yes, but also a close-up look at David's wounds, his worries, and his despair. There is a surprising amount of David's *self* in the Psalms, and that's not a coincidence. For many of us, David included, we cannot raise our gaze to God until we first name our pain, understand it, and begin the work of healing.

It is the kindness and grace of God to us that his Word would include psalms like Psalms 22 and 55 to reassure us of the importance of naming our pain. It reminds us that this sort of self-examination is not selfish but holy and wise.

Whenever we notice me-centered scripts, assumptions, or thoughts spiraling in our minds, it is healthy and prudent to consider whether underneath them all is not simply vanity or pride or sin but an unhealed wound crying out for attention.

If that is what you discover, I invite you to name that pain, study it, understand it, and give yourself time to heal. You cannot forget the self until you first heal the self.

REFLECT: If there are any patterns of insecurity or self-doubt in your life, take some time to dig underneath them. Through prayer or journaling, keep asking the question, "Why do I respond this way?" until you reach the true answer.

Notice Your Narcissism

Only after we genuinely know and accept everything we find within our self can we begin to develop the discernment to know what should be crucified and what should be embraced as an important part of self.

DAVID BENNER

If, then, there is any encouragement in Christ, if any consolation of love, if any fellowship with the Spirit, if any affection and mercy, make my joy complete by thinking the same way, having the same love, united in spirit, intent on one purpose. Do nothing out of selfish ambition or conceit, but in humility consider others as more important than yourselves. Everyone should look not to his own interests, but rather to the interests of others.

Philippians 2:1–4

Narcissism—and its less sinister cousin, vanity—is more complicated than we give it credit for.

In our modern day and age, we often associate narcissism with a clinical pathology, but it has not always been this way. Dating all the way back to the ancient myth of Narcissus, *narcissism* has historically referred to excessive interest in one's own self, and this self-interest appears on a spectrum. Not everyone with narcissistic tendencies has narcissistic personality disorder.

The reasons for a person's narcissism are complex. In his book *When Narcissism Comes to Church*, Chuck DeGroat writes, "I have a working theory that narcissistic pastors are driven by shame."[1] In other words, narcissism may be the symptom of an underlying issue. Still, this dynamic is not simply limited to pastors. Regardless of our career path or personality type, many of us focus on ourselves because our *selves* are in pain, which is why it is so important to notice and name our wounds.

Knowing this, we can have compassion on ourselves in our struggles with narcissism and vanity. The temptation toward self-focus does not make us bad people but can instead mean that some part of us is wounded and in need of care.

However, pain is not the only reason we focus on ourselves. Sometimes we focus on ourselves because of sin.

In my own journey from self-preoccupation to self-forgetfulness, I have had to reckon with the reality that sometimes I am just vain. Sometimes I am arrogant. Sometimes I don't want to put other peoples' interests ahead of my own, because it is easier to put mine first.

And sometimes I do this, not because I am wounded or because I am driven by some deeply buried shame but because I am prideful and slothful and that is what I want to do.

While it is true that some forms of self-focus keep us in bondage and are essentially self-punishing, other forms are deceitfully rewarding. When we make our coworkers do the tasks we hate, when we make our spouse get up with the sick child because we would rather just stay in bed, when we vent the whole truth of our feelings without consideration for the emotional wreckage in our wake, we aren't necessarily acting out of deep-seated pain. Not always. Sometimes we are prioritizing our own comfort, opinions, appearance, or preferences, simply because we want to. And the antidote to this behavior is repentance.

Repentance can be a loaded word. For some of us, it has been wielded and weaponized to condemn and to shame. But as Jesus understood it, repentance meant turning away from death and back to life, and that is no less the case when we are talking about narcissism. In fact, that is the very moral of the story of Narcissus.

If you are unfamiliar with this ancient Greek myth, it tells of a man who falls in love with his own reflection. He is so enamored by his own beauty that he refuses to part with it. Instead, he perches in front of his reflection and stares deeply into his own eyes while minutes turn into hours, hours turn into days, and days turn into weeks. He is so captivated by his own appearance that he does not notice his body wasting away.

Until, ultimately, he dies.

This is where narcissism leads. Not necessarily to physical death but spiritual death. This is why the writers of Scripture warn against the idolatry of the self. It is also why God's Word exhorts us, again and again, to love God and others: It is the message of the first and second greatest commandments, it is the arc of nearly every psalm, and it's embodied in the incarnation.

Prioritizing God and others is one of the dominant themes of Philippians. Over and over, we are invited to shift our gaze off of self and back onto God and others, not because that is what makes us good Christians but because that is what makes us whole.

The human soul was not created for a purpose so small as our selves. Living for the self is like living in a hospital bed: In theory, it's 24/7 attention and care. What better way to thrive?

But in reality, this is not living. It is slowly dying.

You were made for so much more than living for you.

REFLECT: Are there any areas of your life where you prioritize your wants or needs over someone else's? Are there areas where you overly focus on yourself, not because of insecurity but because of vanity, pride, sloth, or selfishness?

DAY 6

Notice Your Identity

If we've invested our sense of self in something small, temporal, and unstable, we will become small, temporal, and unstable people.

HANNAH ANDERSON

When the Lord saw that Leah was neglected, he opened her womb; but Rachel was unable to conceive. Leah conceived, gave birth to a son, and named him Reuben, for she said, "The Lord has seen my affliction; surely my husband will love me now."

She conceived again, gave birth to a son, and said, "The Lord heard that I am neglected and has given me this son also." So she named him Simeon.

She conceived again, gave birth to a son, and said, "At last, my husband will become attached to me because I

have borne three sons for him." Therefore he was named
Levi.

And she conceived again, gave birth to a son, and said,
"This time I will praise the Lord." Therefore she named
him Judah. Then Leah stopped having children.

Genesis 29:31–35

A t first glance, the story of Rachel and Leah does
not seem like a story about self-focus. It seems
like a story about two scoundrel men and the
women they mistreated.

We first meet Rachel and Leah in Genesis 29, when
Jacob encounters Rachel and immediately falls in love
with her. Jacob—who is well known for having betrayed
his older brother by stealing his birthright—is a dishonest
trickster, but he meets his match in Rachel's father, Laban.
As soon as Laban discovers Jacob's interest in Rachel, he
recognizes a financial opportunity and uses Rachel as
a bargaining chip. Laban will allow Jacob to marry his
daughter on one condition: Jacob must work for Laban
for seven years.

Jacob agrees to these terms, but at the end of his seven-
year commitment, Laban tricks him into marrying Rachel's
sister, Leah, instead. How did this young man manage to
marry the wrong woman? Great question! I suspect he was
not looking at her *face*, if you know what I mean. But because of this inexplicable mistake, Jacob is forced to work
another seven years in order to marry Rachel.

By the end of this whole matrimonial shakedown, Jacob is married to both sisters, but his heart belongs to only one: Rachel.

Of course, this puts Leah in a terrible spot. She is a third wheel in an arranged marriage. Nothing about this situation echoes the goodness God intended for marriage, but Leah is not alone in her suffering. Rachel has challenges of her own. Unlike Leah, who quickly has many children, Rachel is barren, which means she is also processing the pain of being "not enough" for her husband.

Both women are suffering, and their heartaches could have formed a bridge of connection to one another. Unfortunately, that is not what occurs. Rather than console one another or care for one another in their respective devastations, these sisters compete. In fact, Leah views her sister's infertility as an opportunity to gain favor with Jacob, and she begins having children as if her value depends on it. Notice the names she gives her boys and what each name symbolizes:

Reuben. *Seen.*
Simeon. *Heard.*
Levi. *Attached.*

Each one of these names expresses a deep longing in Leah's heart: to be seen, to be heard, to be attached to. With the birth of each successive child, she yearns to be acknowledged and treasured by Jacob in these very particular ways. But what this naming also means—what Leah is *really* doing here—is *using* these boys. She is depending on them to fill her, to dignify her, and to give her worth.

In short, she is making these boys a part of her identity. She is making these boys' lives *about her.*

This particular form of self-preoccupation is what we are left with anytime we find our identity in something other than Christ. Whether we derive our value from our children, our marriage, our accomplishments, our work, our possessions, or even our calling, we take good and beautiful gifts intended to glorify our Father in heaven, and we make them very, very small.

When we do this—when we orient the gifts of God toward ourselves instead of toward him—we strip them of their meaning and power in our lives. We hollow out their purpose, which is why they ultimately fail to satisfy us. Even worse, when we do this to *people,* as Leah does with her sons, we cease to have a healthy, intimate relationship because we are not actually seeing them. We are seeing only ourselves.

Thankfully, this is not the end of Leah's story. In verse 35, Leah stops relying on these boys for her identity, and instead she raises her gaze. She names her fourth son Judah, saying, "This time I will praise the LORD."

That statement is the sound of chains breaking. Leah is now free from making her sons' lives about her, free from relying on them to prop up her identity. The same freedom is available to us. Whenever we find our identity in anything other than Christ, we direct it toward too small a thing.

But as Leah's story reminds us, it is never too late to raise our gaze.

REFLECT: Where are you tempted to anchor your identity? Do you notice any particular ways you are making that area of your life about you instead of about God and others?

Notice Your False Self

Every one of us is shadowed by an illusory person: a false self.

This is the man that I want myself to be but who cannot exist, because God does not know anything about him. And to be unknown of God is altogether too much privacy.

My false and private self is the one who wants to exist outside the reach of God's will and God's love—outside of reality and outside of life. And such a self cannot help but be an illusion.

THOMAS MERTON

Then Jesus said to the Jews who had believed him, "If you continue in my word, you really are my disciples. You will know the truth, and the truth will set you free."

John 8:31–32

I have often heard it said that you cannot deny the self until you first have a self. This is, in fact, the first stage of self-forgetfulness: affirming the goodness of the self and healing and restoring it so that you are not so distracted by your own pain that you can't see anything else.

However, we cannot do this healing work if we don't have access to our self in the first place. Many of us walk around the world with a kind of armor on, one that protects us from being fully known by others but also prevents us from being fully known by ourselves.

That armor is called the "false self."

Theologian and mystic Thomas Merton wrote of this false self in his book *New Seeds of Contemplation*. The false self, as he described it, is the self we present to the world. When we walk into the room, it is the image that we think people want us to be.

The false self presents itself when we are asked a professional question we don't know the answer to and, rather than confess our lack of knowledge, make something up.

This is the self that exaggerates our accomplishments to seem impressive to those around us.

This is the self that buries our anger or hurt feelings, because we think being a good Christian means being nice all the time.

This is the self that lies in order to hide failures, shortcomings, or vices.

This self is always contorting and striving to be accepted and embraced, because—as Merton so insightfully notes—there is no grace for the false self. There can be no grace for someone who doesn't exist. There can be no grace for an illusion of ourselves.

There is only grace for our actual selves.

For too many of us, the true self cannot focus on God, or others, because it is shrouded by the false self. So it's important to name the false self. We must be able to identify the image that we put into the world to hide our weaknesses and limitations, and once we do this, we can put the armor away and invite God to do his healing work in us.

REFLECT: Take some time right now to consider your false self. When you walk into a room, who do you become (depending on the room)? What are some of your false self's defaults or defense mechanisms?

Do You Want to Get Well?

Change happens when the pain of staying the same is greater than the pain of change.

TONY ROBBINS

By the Sheep Gate in Jerusalem there is a pool, called Bethesda in Aramaic, which has five colonnades. Within these lay a large number of the disabled—blind, lame, and paralyzed.

One man was there who had been disabled for thirty-eight years. When Jesus saw him lying there and realized he had already been there a long time, he said to him, "Do you want to get well?"

"Sir," the disabled man answered, "I have no one to put me into the pool when the water is stirred up, but while I'm coming, someone goes down ahead of me."

"Get up," Jesus told him, "pick up your mat and walk." Instantly the man got well, picked up his mat, and started to walk.

John 5:2–9

D o you want to get well?"
This is perhaps one of the most haunting and soul-searching questions that Jesus asks anyone in the Gospels. He poses this question to a man who is disabled and lying near the pool of Bethesda because, as legend had it, an angel would descend and "stir" the waters of the pool. Whoever was the first to enter the water after it had been stirred would be healed, which is why the man was positioned near this particular pool: He wanted to get well.

Why, then, would Jesus ask this question?

Because the question is rhetorical. Like every other rhetorical question that Jesus asks, the goal is not to get an answer but to illuminate something in the hearer's heart. Jesus is inviting the man to see himself honestly, because there exists inside this man something that exists in every one of us: a contradiction.

Like the man in John 5, most of us are well acquainted with our wounds. If we were asked if we wanted to be healed, we would answer yes without hesitation. And yet, that isn't always the truth. Sometimes we do not want to be healed, because our pain has become our identity.

Sometimes our pain—our rejection, our failure, our loneliness, our wound—has become the story we tell ourselves about ourselves. It is a story in which we are both the hero and the victim. Every setback, every slight, every negative experience (and sometimes even the positive ones) is conformed to this single script. Maybe it gives us a twisted sense of self-righteousness, or maybe we simply don't know who we are without it, but we are choosing to wallow in unforgiveness, isolation, and toxic pride, rather than heal.

Of course, some of us *do* want to be healed. We are working on ourselves, but healing takes time, so our lack of healing is not indicative of a lack of faith. But for many of us, we cannot move forward without first asking ourselves this question, because some of us want the pity party. We are not prepared to let go of the me-centered scripts in which we are special but in the very worst way. For reasons we may not even fully understand, we want to be the martyr, the put-upon, the never-invited-and-always-left-out.

And I will be the first to confess that I am chief among sinners.

But if we want to be healed of our insecurities and self-doubt, if we want to be set free of the bondage of self, we have a role to play in our own deliverance. It takes courage and humility and dying to self, but it is the only path to actual healing.

So, my question for you—Jesus's question for you—is this: Do you want to be well?

Do you *actually* want to be free?

Do you *actually* want to be secure?

Do you *actually* want to be healed?

Or, when push comes to shove, will you settle back into the learned helplessness of the familiar?

Only you can answer those questions honestly, but once you are *actually* ready to receive your full inheritance in Christ, Jesus invites you to do something surprising. The God of the universe—the all-powerful miracle maker and overcomer of sin and death, the God who does not need you to help him in the least—invites you to participate in your own healing.

Or, as Jesus puts it to the man in John 5:8, "Pick up your mat and walk."

Not because your healing depends on human effort, but because in the process of bringing about whatever good thing he is up to, he almost always prefers to include you.

REFLECT: Do you want to get well? If so, what has God taught you in the waiting? If your honest answer is no, what is holding you back?

Movement 2

RECEIVING
YOUR
TRUE SELF

The Elusive True Self

A self is not something static, tied up in a pretty parcel and handed to the child, finished and complete. A self is always becoming.

MADELEINE L'ENGLE

> For it was you who created my inward parts;
> you knit me together in my mother's womb.
> I will praise you
> because I have been remarkably and wondrously
>   made.
> Your works are wondrous,
> and I know this very well.
> My bones were not hidden from you
> when I was made in secret,
> when I was formed in the depths of the earth.
> Your eyes saw me when I was formless;

> all my days were written in your book and planned
> before a single one of them began.
>
> Psalm 139:13–16

Those of us originally from the Western world belong to a culture obsessed with finding our "true self." If our culture had a secular gospel, this would be it—the gospel of the true self: "If you are struggling with discontentment, boredom, insecurity, shame, or a lack of passion for your work, it is because you are not living from your true self."

Of course, there is a lot of truth to this. When we are more in tune with our false selves than our true selves, we are absolutely going to wrestle with shame, insecurity, and self-doubt, because our acceptance is conditional upon our ability to perform. The false self's confidence is precarious and fragile.

At the same time, our culture's definition of the true self is equally unstable and also subjective. There is no common measure of what constitutes the true self or how to know when we have found it. It is also unclear how the true self relates to various stages of life. Are you more or less your true self if you have to take a job you don't like or if you stop working to care for a family member?

Adding even more confusion is the influence of social media, platforms designed to showcase the false self under the guise of the true. An individual may present themselves as living their best authentic lives, but it's impossible to know whether this is actually true (and very often, it is not). As a result, you might log on to social media and get the impression that everyone has found their true selves except you.

Because of the elusive nature of the true self, it does not always deliver what it promises. It does not yield the peace and resilient confidence we assume that it will. This is also what distinguishes the gospel of the true self from the gospel of Jesus Christ.

Pastor Tim Keller once said that the Christian identity is "received, not achieved."[1] In contrast with the squishy identity offered by our culture, Jesus gives us a fixed point toward which we are aiming: himself. The more we become like him, the more we become our true selves. Or as theologian C. S. Lewis once put it, "The more we get what we now call 'ourselves' out of the way and let Him take us over, the more truly ourselves we become."[2]

It is a bit of a paradox—that we find our true selves by aiming at Christ—but it also makes sense. We will be our truest selves, not the false self that performs in order to gain acceptance or to hide its wounds, when we are operating out of our identity as wholly accepted and loved. We will no longer contort our God-given selves in order to belong, because we already do. To put on the identity of Christ is to put on the identity of a child of the King and wear it like a robe. We are still our unique selves—with our own talents, passions, and perspectives—but we're set free from the diminishing and disfiguring effects of sin.

When God had you in mind at the foundations of the world, he loved you even then. He created you because it brought him delight, and your true self, made in his image, is an expression of his goodness and his love. While your self has been marred by sin, the sin is not who you are. Not at your core. And it is not who you were created to be.

While you may not know who your true self is, you can be sure that God already does. He has known it since the beginning of time, and through Christ, he is restoring you to it day by day. Simply open your hands and receive.

REFLECT: What has been your understanding of your true self? Is it a question you ask yourself often, or never? Have you found your true self to be elusive, or do you feel confident about who God created you to be in Christ?

You Are Made
in the Image of God

There is something previous to what I think about myself,
and it is what God thinks of me.

EUGENE PETERSON

Then God said, "Let us make man in our image, according to our likeness. They will rule the fish of the sea, the
birds of the sky, the livestock, the whole earth, and the
creatures that crawl on the earth."

So God created man
in his own image;
he created him in the image of God;
he created them male and female.

Genesis 1:26–27

Which part of you—your talents, your interests, your personality—most reflects God?

Have you ever considered this question before? I suspect we are all well aware of the parts of ourselves that do *not* reflect God, but Genesis 1 and 2 remind us that to be a human is to be made in the image of our Creator. Each of our beings tells a story about who God is and what he is like, and that story is vast and mosaic. We are, after all, reflecting the image of an *infinite* God, an impossible task for finite beings like you and me without the help of God. But together, each one of us points to something true and beautiful and eternal.

So again I ask: Which part of you reflects the image of God?

The answer is all of you.

Of course, every part of you is marred by sin, but that fact does not alter your fundamental identity. An apple tree that has stopped bearing fruit is still an apple tree, and so it is with human nature. Even if our faculties decline with age, we are no less human. With this in mind, let's consider a few aspects of yourself that, as Scripture tells us, reflect the One who created you.

Your Mind

Whether you are logical or creative, organized or visionary, your mind reflects the mind of God. After all, it is God who imagined the world into being, ordered creation, and then dispatched his Son—the "Word" or "logos" of God (John 1:1), literally his "logic"—into the world. God is neither left-brained nor right-brained, neither partial to sciences nor humanities. He is all. Which means your way of thinking and seeing the world—your perspectives, your insights, your dreams—do not simply tell us about you but also about the God who made you.

Your Emotions

For much of human history, emotions have been treated as a weakness rather than a strength, even within the church. But Scripture tells a different story. God is, quite often, full of emotion. He experiences compassion, sorrow, wrath, and joy, and these emotions "move" him. He is not mastered by his emotions, but they play a mysterious and important role in his intervention in the world. Likewise, our emotions are not a hindrance to holiness or wisdom. In fact, when we consider our emotions rather than ignore them, we can become more like God.

Your Body

When God became human, he had a body. This same body died, was buried, and was resurrected, and when Jesus ascended to heaven, he did so bodily.

There is no greater affirmation of the goodness of the body than this. What makes you *YOU* is not simply your soul housed in a body. Your body is as much "you" as your heart and your mind, which is why God intends to redeem it too. Your body reflects the image of the God who once walked this earth in a body, and your body is good.

Mind. Emotions. Body.

Each of these aspects of yourself bears the image of God, and there is no part of you that mirrors him more or less. And, as finite creatures reflecting the infinite God, there is no single way to reflect him. Each of us "images" him uniquely.

As you consider who God created you to be, and how your specific "self" reflects him, ask yourself a different question: "Does my image of myself, and my treatment of myself, match the God-given truth about myself?"

REFLECT: Consider which part of yourself you like the least. This could be a physical trait or a personality trait. How does this aspect of yourself reflect the image of God?

You Are a Child of God

When Eve thought of God as something less than father, that means she also thought of herself as something less than daughter.

TYLER STATON

When he came to his senses, he said, "How many of my father's hired workers have more than enough food, and here I am dying of hunger! I'll get up, go to my father, and say to him, 'Father, I have sinned against heaven and in your sight. I'm no longer worthy to be called your son. Make me like one of your hired workers.'" So he got up and went to his father. But while the son was still a long way off, his father saw him and was filled with compassion. He ran, threw his arms around his neck, and kissed him.

Luke 15:17–20

My parents are two of the most generous people I have ever known. They have given me everything I could have asked for and more. Support, encouragement, opportunities, a happy home. I've had it all. And yet, of all the many things they have given me in my life, by far the greatest is this: the kind of love that makes God's love for me imaginable.

It is not difficult for me to conceive of what my heavenly Father's love is like because my earthly parents modeled it so faithfully. Throughout my life, my parents have pursued me, helped me, forgiven me, and served me, even when it cost them greatly. I have never wondered if they were proud of me or if I could do anything to negate their love for me. I rest secure in an unbreakable bond that has steadied me through many of the storms of life.

My identity as the daughter of Rich and Debbie Hodde has been a source of comfort, security, confidence, joy, and peace, because I know I am both treasured and held.

How much more are we treasured and held as sons and daughters of God?

Unfortunately, not everyone's story is like mine. For many people, their parents' love was *very* conditional. Instead of love, some received abuse. When this is our story, the love of the Father is far more difficult to grasp, which means our identity as his children is difficult to grasp as well. It is one thing to be told you are a child of God but quite another to live like it.

Thankfully, Jesus knew this would be difficult, which is why he tells so many stories about what the Father's love is like. One of the most well-known is the parable of the prodigal son, a story about a young man who grows up with parents much like mine. This son wants for nothing. His father delights in giving him everything, even granting his inheritance before it is time. If that is what the son asks for, the father is going to grant it.

The son, however, does not reciprocate. He is more interested in his father's wealth than his father's love. He takes the inheritance money and spends it all. When a famine hits the land, the son becomes so destitute that he envies the pigs he is feeding to make a meager sum. He yearns to go home, but he also worries that he is too late. Surely, his identity as his father's son has been erased.

The son thinks this only because he does not understand what it means to be a dad.

Good parents—healthy parents—never stop loving their kids. They never stop pursuing their kids, supporting their kids, fighting for their kids, or waiting for their kids. Good parents never even stop thinking about their kids, because good parents would do literally anything— would *give* literally anything—to see their kids thriving and whole.

And God is not simply a good parent. He is the best.

A lot is at stake when we forget whose we are. When we live as if we belong to no one, as if we are not children of the most generous Father, as if we are not treasured and held, then our focus will be small and selfward by necessity. If no one is looking out for us, then we have to look out for ourselves.

But if you are in Christ, that is not who you are. Your identity is not "daughter of a father who left," or "son of a mother who wouldn't stop drinking." Your identity is not "rejected," "orphaned," or "abused." Your identity is not even "child of wonderful, loving parents." When you are born again, you receive a new family name—"child of God"—and *that* identity is who you are.

Your identity, who you *are*, is a child of God, which means you do not have to live as if you are all alone in the world, and you don't have to live as if you are the only one looking out for you.

Someone else already has that job.

REFLECT: Our identities are often defined in relation to other people (spouse, children, parents, etc.). What relationships in your life most inform your identity?

You Are in Christ

When I hear a Christian say, "I'm just a sinner saved by grace," I want to say, "That makes as much sense as a butterfly saying, 'I'm just a worm with wings.'"

JAMES BRYAN SMITH

I have been crucified with Christ, and I no longer live, but Christ lives in me. The life I now live in the body, I live by faith in the Son of God, who loved me and gave himself for me.

Galatians 2:20

Years ago, when my husband and I were working on our PhDs, we spent four years living in Chicago. If you have never been, Chicago is beautiful, the people are welcoming, and the food is delicious. We loved it there.

The only problem? The winters.

I am a Southern girl through and through, and those winters were for the birds. When it was forty degrees below zero, or when it was still snowing in May, I would daydream about running away to Florida. One of the only ways I survived was by wearing a thick down coat that extended all the way to my knees, and I lived in that coat.

These days, I am back in North Carolina, where the winters are mild and the summers are humid. This is my sort of climate. I still own that coat, and I still wear it on especially cold days, but it mostly sits in my closet as a memento from a previous season of my life.

Imagine, for a moment, if I wore that coat all the time—not just during the winter but during the summer also. Although it kept me warm during those Chicago winters, it would not serve me during North Carolina summers. Not only would it make me uncomfortable but, if I wore it in the sweltering heat for long, it could downright harm me.

There are few concepts that are harder to grasp than that of "identity," but this is especially true for understanding our identity "in Christ." How can you still be you when Paul tells us it is "no longer you who live, but Christ who lives in you" (Gal. 2:20, paraphrased)?

Scripture draws on quite a few metaphors to capture this divine mystery, but the one that has helped me most is that of "putting on Christ," as one might put on a robe. Or a coat.

This language comes to us in multiple places in the New Testament. In Ephesians 4:22, we are invited to "put off" or "take off" the old self, and then in Romans 13:14, Paul exhorts us to "put on" or "clothe" ourselves in Christ. This metaphor, like all metaphors, has its limits, but it captures a delicate balance represented in Scripture: Putting on the identity of Christ is not a loss of self. Instead, it is the self *enrobed*.

We can think about identity as the clothing that we put on, and sometimes these identities—similar to my winter coat—are necessary. Some of us put on identities of toughness or humor as defense mechanisms in chaotic home environments. They protect us for a time. But at some point, we don't need them anymore, and they can even harm us.

They can also keep our true selves hidden from others—and even from ourselves.

When we make the decision to follow Jesus, it is not an invitation to abandon the self but to clothe ourselves in a new identity. And much like the royal vestments placed on a king at his coronation, these new clothes are not mere adornments; they signal a change in *status*. When Jesus places his mantle upon our shoulders, we are now chosen, adopted, beloved, and redeemed children of the King. We are so entirely clothed in the righteousness of Christ that when God looks at us, he sees his Son.

And also, you are still you.

You are you, wearing heavenly clothes that fit you better than any clothes have ever fit before. Clothes that do not obscure your true self or help you hide in shame. These clothes do not distance you from your true self or pressure you to perform. They most certainly do not serve your hypocrisy. Instead, they elevate your standing; accentuate your best, God-given qualities; make you feel at home in yourself; and dress you for life in eternity. They are able to do all this because they are not just clothes. They are an expression of your identity.

You are still you. But now, you are you *in Christ*.

REFLECT: What "old clothes" or old identities feel comfortable to wear but need to be "put off"?

You Are Beloved

Over the years, I have come to realize that the greatest trap in our life is not success, popularity, or power, but self-rejection.

HENRI NOUWEN

When Jesus was baptized, he went up immediately from the water. The heavens suddenly opened for him, and he saw the Spirit of God descending like a dove and coming down on him. And a voice from heaven said, "This is my beloved Son, with whom I am well-pleased."

Matthew 3:16–17

Grasping and accepting the unconditional love of God are some of the most basic elements of the Christian faith.

And yet, somehow, they're also some of the hardest.

We are, at our core, strivers. Deep down, we are convinced we must do *something* to earn our standing. Or we must make amends for all the ways we have failed. This mindset is so entrenched that we don't even recognize when it is driving us. Rarely, if ever, do I actively think, *I need to be a good enough Christian to be accepted by God and others*, and yet so often I feel the weight of that lie driving my choices. I feel the stress, anxiety, and insecurity of trying to prove myself, of always wondering where I stand.

This never-ending mode of earning is arguably the default setting of humanity. If we are not intentional about remembering how loved we are by God, we will slip into seeking approval.

Why?

In large part, because of a misplaced identity.

Identity is, in the simplest terms, how we see ourselves—or how we want others to see us—and this matters because our identity is also the seat of our operations. A person's identity is the version of themselves that is calling the shots in their lives. If, for example, your primary identity is that of a parent, or a high achiever, or a kid who never felt accepted by their parents, that identity is going to influence what you prioritize and why. Our identity is, for that reason, incredibly powerful and determinative of how we operate in the world. If our identity is misplaced, it can have catastrophic consequences for our lives, so it is no coincidence that the first thing God does, prior to Jesus launching his earthly ministry, is validate Jesus's identity.

In Matthew 3, notice that God declares his love and approval of Jesus *before* Jesus has done a single thing. Jesus has not taught, healed, performed miracles, or suffered on a cross. He has not completed his assignment or even started it. And yet, the Father affirms Jesus as his "beloved Son" (v. 17).

This identity—as the beloved Son of God—will be Jesus's seat of operations. Everything he does from this moment forward will be guided by this title.

For those of you who follow Jesus, this declaration lays claim to your identity as well. From the moment you profess faith in Christ, the truest thing about you is not that you are married, have children, or are really good at your job. The truest thing about you is not that you are divorced or rejected or alone. The truest thing about you is not your gender, your sexual orientation, or how you identify. The truest thing about you is not the trauma from your past or that you recently failed, again.

The truest thing about you is that you are loved by God.

This title of belovedness is meant to be the seat of operations for each and every follower of Jesus. It sets us free from earning, because we don't have to earn what we already have.

If you find yourself wrestling with identity, especially as your stage of life shifts or your health declines, receive the identity that is already yours in Christ. You do not have to "find it" or earn it or perform to gain it. The truest thing about you is that you are loved by God and, no matter what comes, that identity will always remain.

REFLECT: Are you tempted to operate out of some other identity besides your belovedness? What identity is it?

DAY 14

You Are Gifted

For just as the body is one and has many parts, and all the parts of that body, though many, are one body—so also is Christ. . . . Indeed, the body is not one part but many. If the foot should say, "Because I'm not a hand, I don't belong to the body," it is not for that reason any less a part of the body. And if the ear should say, "Because I'm not an eye, I don't belong to the body," it is not for that reason any less a part of the body. If the whole body were an eye, where would the hearing be? If the whole body were an ear, where would the sense of smell be? But as it is, God has arranged each one of the parts in the body just as he wanted.

1 Corinthians 12:12, 14–18

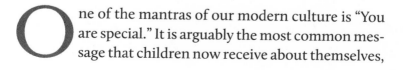 ne of the mantras of our modern culture is "You are special." It is arguably the most common message that children now receive about themselves,

and there is good reason for that. In many ways, it is true. It is even biblical.

But it is also incomplete. The way we use the word "special" is burdened with expectation. If you are special, there is a sense in which you have something to live up to. This designation also offers a false promise of the sort of life you are destined to lead. To repeatedly be told "you are special" means your life will be anything but ordinary, and this is where a worldly understanding of the term and a theological interpretation of it depart.

Scripture describes each one of us as being created with intention and purpose. We are uniquely formed and beloved by God, which means no one can replace us in the Father's heart. And yet the point of this truth is not simply to reinforce our self-esteem or forecast an extraordinary life. Our uniqueness was given to us for a very specific purpose: to build the church.

This is the language Paul uses in 1 Corinthians 12. He describes the church as a body with many parts, and each part plays a necessary role. No part can replace any other part, and no part is more or less important than others. We are an interdependent body, so if one member fails to play its part well, the entire body suffers.

This metaphor equips us with a more biblical understanding of being "special," because it infuses our uniqueness with urgency. Each of us has a unique combination of interests and talents, shaped by our personal stories and experiences, all of which prepare us to fill a singular role in the church. When we do not steward our gifts, the body of Christ is weaker for it.

To be "special" in the kingdom of God may not look the same as being "special" in the world. Our life may appear rather unremarkable to anyone looking in. But faithfulness has nothing to do with noteworthiness and everything to do with the stewardship of what we have been given.

How, then, do we determine our specific "role" in the body of Christ? How can we identify our gifts, and what it is about us that is unique and wonderful and needed?

There are two simple ways to assess this:

First, ask friends and family who love Jesus and know you and who are wise and discerning. Then take their answers seriously. Too often we dismiss positive feedback as if it is mere flattery. "They are just being nice," we assume. But this feedback is how God calls his people; it's the Holy Spirit speaking through others. In view of this truth, receive their feedback not as empty praise but as sacred clues to how God made you.

Second, pay attention to what you enjoy. For some reason, we have it in our heads that work must not be spiritual if it is fun. We think we have to suffer and sacrifice for our actions to be godly, and this is a fundamental misunderstanding of God. It is also a poor theology of work. Suffering will come—make no mistake—but the activities we most enjoy also tell us about how God designed us.

Of course, selfish motives and vain ambitions can sully any calling that God places on our lives, and that is why we practice self-denial. But before we get to that work, we must first be able to answer the question of *what* God created us for in the first place. The answer itself is simple—to love God and others—but how and in what way?

The answers to those questions depend on *you*.

REFLECT: What feedback have you received about yourself in the past? What gifts, or personality traits, have people identified in you? What do they tell you about yourself?

You Are Filled
with the Holy Spirit

Formation into the image of Jesus isn't something we *do* as much as it's something that is done *to* us, by God himself, as we yield to his work of transforming grace. Our job is mostly to make ourselves available.

JOHN MARK COMER

Now there are different gifts, but the same Spirit. There are different ministries, but the same Lord. And there are different activities, but the same God works all of them in each person. A manifestation of the Spirit is given to each person for the common good: to one is given a message of wisdom through the Spirit, to another, a message of knowledge by the same Spirit, to another, faith by the same Spirit, to another, gifts of healing by the one Spirit, to another, the performing of miracles, to another, prophecy, to another, distinguishing between spirits, to another, different kinds of tongues, to another, interpretation of tongues. One and the same Spirit is active in all these, distributing to each person as he wills.

1 Corinthians 12:4–11

I have good news for you: The work of finding your true self is not, ultimately, your job. Nor is the work of becoming your best self. Although we play an important role in our ongoing sanctification and spiritual growth, we cannot achieve either on our own.

That is, in fact, the entire message of the Old Testament: When presented with God's design for creation and his ideals for humanity, we could not live up to the standard. We failed again and again.

And we continue to fall short today. Without the intervention of God, there will always be a gap between who he designed us to be and who we actually are—and that gap is sin.

Thankfully, it isn't ultimately up to us to close that gap. In John 14:16, Jesus promises his disciples that he is sending an "advocate" to help them keep his commands (NIV). This advocate, the Holy Spirit, is who we rely on to transform us into the image of Jesus. The Holy Spirit also makes us more ourselves, as our sin and flesh and self-centered motives lose their stranglehold on our identity.

One of the signs of this transformation at work is the presence of spiritual gifts. In addition to our God-given personalities and interests, the Holy Spirit bestows us with spiritual gifts such as teaching, prophecy, wisdom, knowledge, healing, and faith. These also serve the upbuilding of the church and are given to us not for our own glory, but for God's.

We do not earn our spiritual gifts but receive them. This means that part of discovering our true selves includes discovering our spiritual gifts, and the best way to discern these gifts is the same way we discern other clues about how God created us: asking our community, who know us best.

That said, there is one aspect of spiritual gifts that is very difficult to grasp, especially as it relates to our identity. Because our spiritual gifts are a fruit of the Spirit, not the flesh, they may not always feel as if they belong to us. Not truly. In fact, it is not uncommon for followers of Jesus to experience imposter syndrome regarding their spiritual gifts. We might be known for gifts like hospitality, or mercy, or powerful teaching, while secretly worrying we have everyone fooled. Many of us experience this imposter syndrome because we know our weaknesses full well. The "gift" people see in us feels like a facade. Or, at the very least, a half-truth.

If you can relate to this sort of thinking or if you feel like a hypocrite when someone commends your spiritual gifts—you are not alone in feeling this way.

There is also a sense in which you are right. Your spiritual gifts are *not* a result of your own work. That is to say, they do not originate in you. What people are seeing in you is the Holy Spirit at work in you.

Our spiritual gifts are both "us" and "not us." The Holy Spirit assigns gifts to each of us, which then manifest somewhat uniquely through us, depending on our stories and personalities. That is what makes our spiritual gifts distinctly ours. Distinctly *us*.

Whether your spiritual gifts make you feel like an imposter or you have received them with delight, they are no more or less a part of God's plan for your life and his vision of your "true self." It matters less how you feel about them and more how you steward them for the upbuilding of the church and the "common good" (v. 7). Remember, your gifts are not about you.

REFLECT: Below is a brief list of spiritual gifts. Circle any that have been identified in you and then talk with God about how you are stewarding those gifts.

administration

apostleship

craftsmanship

discernment

evangelism

exhortation

faith

giving

healing

helps

hospitality

intercession

knowledge

leadership

mercy

pastoring/shepherding

prophecy

serving

speaking in tongues

teaching

wisdom

Movement 3

DENYING THE SELF

DAY 16

What It Means to Deny the Self

The spiritual journey is not a career or a success story. It is a series of humiliations of the false self.

THOMAS KEATING

> Then he said to them all, "If anyone wants to follow after me, let him deny himself, take up his cross daily, and follow me. For whoever wants to save his life will lose it, but whoever loses his life because of me will save it."
>
> Luke 9:23–24

In this passage from the Gospel of Luke, Jesus warns his disciples that following him will be difficult. It will entail pain and suffering and loss, which is why he chastens them to deny themselves, take up their cross daily, and follow him. All of which raises an important question: *What does it mean to deny the self?*

The answer to this question matters, because there are a great many misunderstandings about this phrase, which have resulted in a great many misapplications.

Chief among them is the belief that the self is *bad*.

Many of us have heard, or have been taught, that the self is a hindrance to our spiritual growth. Because of this, many Christians see the self as our enemy. We believe we must overcome the self and all its worldly trappings in order to become like Christ. In fact, I once heard a Christian author describe spiritual maturity as the self "disappearing" so that "God might be all."

Of course, there is *some* truth to those sentiments. In John 3:30, John the Baptist states, "He must increase, but I must decrease." And in Romans 7:15, Paul is waging an all-out war with himself when he laments, "I do not understand what I do. For what I want to do I do not do, but what I hate I do" (NIV).

In both of these instances, the self seems like an enemy or an obstacle to overcome. If that is the case, then it's no wonder Jesus instructs us to deny it!

However, this interpretation has one problem: the self is not bad. The self is good. We know this because the self was created in the very image of God. The self has been damaged by the effects of sin, but it will ultimately be fully healed and redeemed in the resurrection.

In her book *The Best of You*, psychologist Dr. Alison Cook offers a helpful explanation of "self-denial" by drawing a distinction between "selfhood" and "selfishness." She defines "selfhood" as being essential to our identity, our "God-given, image-bearing self." "Selfishness," on the other hand, is a prioritizing of the self above all else. This relationship to the self is one of idolatry, because the self is master instead of Christ.[1]

Cook argues that Jesus is referring to this latter relationship to the self—the idolatrous one—when he instructs his disciples to deny themselves and follow him. He is not saying that the self is evil or bad. He is not advising them to devalue the image of God in themselves, or to neglect stewarding the identities they have been given.

Instead, Jesus is teaching his disciples to pursue a *rightly ordered* love of the self, because it is good and healthy and biblical to love the self. In fact, Jesus assumes the goodness of loving ourselves when he tells his followers to love their neighbors *as themselves* (Mark 12:31).

And yet, at the same time, we should not prioritize the self above God and others. True, holy self-forgetfulness cannot exist without this tension. The self is good, and also, we must not idolize it.

Both belong.

Whenever we are thinking about self-denial, we must hold these two truths together. Your self is good and wondrous and reflects the very image of God. God is also committed to making your entire self holy and whole. While Jesus urges each of us to deny the idolatry of self, your self is not your enemy.

Your self is a gift from God.

REFLECT: Spend some time listening to the Spirit and asking if there are any areas of your life in which you are prioritizing your self in unhealthy or disproportionate ways.

DAY 17

Receiving Insecurity

When self is at the center, humiliation feels like an existential threat.

RUSSELL MOORE

The word of the LORD came to me:

> I chose you before I formed you in the womb;
> I set you apart before you were born.
> I appointed you a prophet to the nations.

But I protested, "Oh no, Lord GOD! Look, I don't know how to speak since I am only a youth."
Then the LORD said to me:

> Do not say, "I am only a youth,"
> for you will go to everyone I send you to
> and speak whatever I tell you.
> Do not be afraid of anyone,
> for I will be with you to rescue you.
> This is the LORD's declaration.

Jeremiah 1:4–8

For the longest time, I had only one response to insecurity: fight it.

This was my only response, because it was the only response culture had handed me. Both inside and outside the church, we treat insecurity like a sickness or an attack. We have been taught that whenever we feel insecure, our emotions are lying to us, so our only resort is to launch a counterattack with a barrage of confidence-building affirmations.

Sometimes this is exactly the right response. The experience of being lied to or shamed or abused puts cracks in the foundation of our identities, causing structural damage that needs to be repaired with the love of God and his Word.

But what if our insecurities are not the result of a lie? What if our insecurities are the result of something *true*? What then?

That is the predicament the prophet Jeremiah finds himself in. When God appoints Jeremiah to be his prophet, Jeremiah immediately objects. He is, after all, not yet twenty years old, which is considerably younger than the other prophets in the Old Testament. Historically, God had called much more seasoned men. God called Abraham at seventy-five, Moses at eighty, and Elijah at the relatively younger age of thirty. Jeremiah has neither the life experience nor the leadership experience that this role would require, and because of this, he feels deeply insecure. So much so that he tries to turn down the role.

As we read about Jeremiah's insecurity, here is what we must not miss: Jeremiah is not imagining his shortcomings.

They are very real. He *is* young. It is entirely possible that the people of Israel will use this against him. He is also less experienced than other men, which is a legitimate cause for concern.

Jeremiah's insecurities are actually rooted in something true about him, and this is an important reminder to us all: Sometimes we feel like we are not enough because we are not enough. Sometimes we worry that we are not up to the task because we know that we are not.

Our insecurities are not always rooted in a lie. Sometimes they are a reflection of something that is deeply true and can't be banished with self-affirmations (even biblical ones). But if we have only one response to insecurity—to resist it, to fight back, to bury it with self-help mantras—we lose the opportunity to hear what our insecurity is really saying to us. Usually, it is saying two things:

1. You have reached a human limit. Or, you have reached the end of yourself.
2. You are insecure because your confidence is founded on something insecure. Some part of your identity is resting on a foundation other than Christ.

In other words, insecurity reveals our true spiritual state. Insecurity highlights what our confidence is *actually* founded on, whether it be our outward appearance, our career success, our reputation, or simply our ability to be liked.

If we believe Jesus's words in John 8:32, that "the truth will set [us] free," then we must listen to whatever part of our insecurity is actually restoring us to reality. Whether our insecurity is pointing out a very real limitation that needs to be acknowledged and honored and entrusted to Christ or simply pointing out some part of ourselves that is standing on sand instead of *the* Rock, we deny ourselves the benefit of knowing these truths if our only response is to pray it away.

When insecurity hits, what is often under attack is not our selves but an idol we have wrapped around us so tightly that removing it feels like a death. But what is actually hurting us is not the insecurity; the insecurity is merely the symptom, not the cause.

Our challenge, then, is not to treat the symptom but to welcome the pain as a severe mercy. It is the first necessary step in diagnosing what it is our souls actually need.

REFLECT: Is there an insecurity in your life that is telling you something important or true? It might be helpful to process this with a trusted person who can help you discern the voice of the Spirit from the condemnations of his enemy.

Receiving Humiliation

The kingdom of self is heavily defended territory.

EUGENE PETERSON

Adopt the same attitude as that of Christ Jesus,

>who, existing in the form of God,
>did not consider equality with God
>as something to be exploited.
>Instead he emptied himself
>by assuming the form of a servant,
>taking on the likeness of humanity.
>And when he had come as a man,
>he humbled himself by becoming obedient
>to the point of death—
>even to death on a cross.
>For this reason God highly exalted him
>and gave him the name
>that is above every name,

so that at the name of Jesus
every knee will bow—
in heaven and on earth
and under the earth—
and every tongue will confess
that Jesus Christ is Lord,
to the glory of God the Father.

Philippians 2:5–11

There is a well-known survival mechanism observed in both nature and human psychology called the fight-or-flight response. We exhibit this stress response in the face of danger by either defending ourselves and fighting back or withdrawing and fleeing. This response is one we hold in common with many of our neighbors in the animal kingdom but with one key distinction: For humans, our fight-or-flight response is not solely triggered by the threat of danger. It is also triggered by the threat of humiliation.

You have probably experienced both responses at some time or another, depending on the particular form of embarrassment. Maybe you dodged a former friend at Target, because things ended so awkwardly between you. *Flight*. Or maybe you tumbled down a flight of stairs in front of a crowd of onlookers only to jump up and loudly declare, "I'm fine! I'm fine! Ha, ha, ha," while you were actually dying inside. *Fighting*, desperately, for your dignity.

We have all been there, but it is important to name *why* we have these responses to experiences that pose no actual danger to us. What is endangered through humiliation is not our physical safety but our image. And for some of us that is nearly as precious. Whenever we are disgraced, the person we want to be—or the person we want others to think that we are—faces an existential threat. *That* is what triggers our fight-or-flight response.

Why does this matter?

Very often, we respond to our humiliations (our mistakes, our failures, our shortcomings, our flaws) as if our very selves are under attack. As a result of this perception, we recruit God to our cause. We turn to Scripture and prayer to shield our weaknesses and insecurities (sometimes a wise and fitting response) while never considering whether what is under attack is not our selves but the image we want to project.

We will never see this if we quickly shoo away the discomfort, labeling it "an attack of the enemy." The truth is, regardless of the enemy's schemes, we do not have to fear humiliation.

Why?

Because of Christ.

Philippians 2 reminds us that we can gladly lower ourselves, even when it means we'll experience humiliation, because Jesus turned humiliation into a path back to life. Rather than remain far off in heaven, in all his deserved glory, Jesus lowered himself and took the form of a servant, suffered humiliation and shame, and then redeemed it all in glory, forever changing our relationship with humiliation, failure, and shame.

Furthermore, Jesus did not simply take the teeth out of humiliation; he turned it into his servant. Now our moments of disgrace can become the very tools of our remaking. Rather than destroy us, moments of humiliation can make us more like him—which is to say, more fully alive than we ever were before.

Because of the cross, we no longer have to fear humiliation. Because of the cross, humiliation can be refashioned into a gift. It comes in the ugliest wrapping, but the most wonderful treasure is inside, if we will receive it.

REFLECT: Are there any aspects of your life right now—in your job, your family, or your season of life—where you can receive humiliation rather than fight it?

DAY 19

Receiving Rejection

When Joseph's brothers saw that their father was dead, they said to one another, "If Joseph is holding a grudge against us, he will certainly repay us for all the suffering we caused him."

So they sent this message to Joseph, "Before he died your father gave a command: 'Say this to Joseph: Please forgive your brothers' transgression and their sin—the suffering they caused you.' Therefore, please forgive the transgression of the servants of the God of your father." Joseph wept when their message came to him. His brothers also came to him, bowed down before him, and said, "We are your slaves!"

But Joseph said to them, "Don't be afraid. Am I in the place of God? You planned evil against me; God planned it for good to bring about the present result—the survival of many people. Therefore don't be afraid. I will take care of you and your children." And he comforted them and spoke kindly to them.

Genesis 50:15–21

I have always found the experience of rejection especially exposing.

Prior to a series of romantic and friendship breakups, I had seen myself as valuable, attractive, smart, and fun, but these experiences challenged my self-image. Instead of feeling dignified, I felt pathetic. There were no fig leaves big enough to cover the shame of my rejection. Humiliation was my new name.

Romantic and friendship rejections are among the most painful there are. It's why the entire country music industry is fueled by the pain of unrequited love. Heartbreak has the potential to shake you to your core. But even worse than being rejected by a friend or significant other is being rejected by your own family, and that is exactly what happened to Joseph.

In Genesis 37 we meet Joseph, the favorite son of Jacob. Jacob so shamelessly prefers Joseph to the other boys that he lavishes him with an extravagant, multicolored coat. Unsurprisingly, this does nothing for Joseph's relationship with his brothers. But Joseph doesn't help. At the age of seventeen, he begins receiving dreams where he rules over all of his brothers, and then he foolishly chooses to tell them about the dreams.

Between his favored status in the family and these obnoxious dreams, the brothers eventually become fed up. They ambush Joseph, steal his coat, fake his death, and sell him into slavery.

We all know sibling relationships are complicated, but the cruelty and inhumanity of this rejection reaches a category all its own. At the hands of his brothers, Joseph loses his family, his home, and his status as a treasured son, taking instead the status of a slave. And all of this happens within a matter of days. This is well beyond sibling rivalry.

Rejection is now a part of Joseph's story. And yet, remarkably, this very deep wound does not change the way he sees himself. Rejection is his experience, but it is not his identity. Even though he will encounter more rejections and setbacks, the rejection will never invade his soul or drag his focus inward like an emotional black hole.

That is because rejection—like most humiliations—always presents us with a choice. We can receive the rejection like a new name, pasting it across our foreheads and running every experience through the damaged prism of our greatest betrayal.

Or we can receive rejection as a new place to experience God's grace in our lives.

Again and again, Joseph chooses the latter. Rather than indulge in self-pity or throw up his hands in despair (because truly, if anyone could legitimately make the case that "nothing good ever happens" to him, it would be Joseph!), Joseph trusts that what his brothers planned for evil, God would use for good (see 50:20). And because of this, Joseph's rejection becomes the source of his entire family's redemption.

When we are able to respond similarly, to receive rejection not as a new identity, but as a new place to experience God's grace, we participate with God in telling a better story. When we raise our gaze off of ourselves and onto

Jesus, we can ask, "How might God use this for good?" If we can get to the point of daring to ask this question, it just might become the moment we begin turning our pain into purpose.

REFLECT: When was the last time you experienced rejection? How might you turn that pain into purpose?

Receiving Exclusion

> After this, Jesus went out and saw a tax collector named
> Levi sitting at the tax office, and he said to him, "Follow
> me." So, leaving everything behind, he got up and began
> to follow him.
>
> Then Levi hosted a grand banquet for him at his
> house. Now there was a large crowd of tax collectors and
> others who were reclining at the table with them. But
> the Pharisees and their scribes were complaining to his
> disciples, "Why do you eat and drink with tax collectors
> and sinners?"
>
> Jesus replied to them, "It is not those who are healthy
> who need a doctor, but those who are sick. I have not
> come to call the righteous, but sinners to repentance."
>
> Luke 5:27–32

W hy wasn't I invited?"
    It is humbling to admit I still ask this ques-
tion regularly. Whether it's a baby shower my

friends attended without me or a conference I wasn't asked to speak at, the familiar sting of exclusion still visits me regularly.

As it does for us all.

In his sermon titled "The Inner Ring," C. S. Lewis explains how many of us yearn to be included in one social "ring" or another: "I believe that in all men's lives at certain periods, and in many men's lives at all periods between infancy and extreme old age, one of the most dominant elements is the desire to be inside the local Ring and the terror of being left outside."[1]

The strange thing about exclusion is that it is a universal experience, and still, it feels so personal when it happens to us. When we're left out, the very first question that springs to our minds is "Why wasn't *I* included?" Notice that we do *not* ask, "Why wasn't this other person included?" The offense feels targeted at us. We rarely stop to ask, "Why wasn't this other woman invited to the baby shower, even though she is much better friends with that group than I am?" Or, "Why wasn't this other speaker invited to the conference, even though she is a much better communicator than me?"

No, the first question is always a me-centered one.

This is the temptation of exclusion, as painful as it is. The "ring" from which we are excluded eclipses everything else. It's all we can see. It blinds us to the reality that, very often, we are *not* alone.

It also blinds us to the reality that true belonging does not come from inclusion in any ring. Until we find belonging in Jesus, we will spend a lifetime trying to gain access to an endless series of rings.

If we welcome exclusion when it comes, rather than ruminate over why we were singled out in a me-centered spiral, we can develop eyes to see others who are excluded too. It can also instill in us an urgency not to exclude.

All of which brings us to this story in Luke 5. Verses 31–32 are the most well-known (and arguably most memorable) sentences in this story, but because of that, it's easy to miss the significance of what has just happened. Tax collectors were often Jews employed by the Roman government, which is why they were considered traitors. They prioritized personal profit and advancement over God and his people. This is why the Gospels often mention them alongside "sinners" (Matt. 9:10; Mark 2:15).

Unsurprisingly, tax collectors were excluded people. One might argue that they brought this status on themselves, but that only makes Levi's transformation all the more remarkable. After only a brief encounter with Jesus, Levi changes from a villainous outcast to an extravagant includer. Luke 5:29 tells us that shortly after being invited to follow Jesus, he hosts a banquet for other sinners like himself, which indicates that his purpose has shifted. He is no longer looking out for himself alone or sitting on the margins looking in. Rather than hoard Jesus's attention, he adopts Jesus's vision. He now sees the way Jesus sees. He now has the eyes to see others who are excluded too.

This is always the opportunity of exclusion: Jesus can transform it into a mission. Whenever we accept our belonging in Christ, we are released from elbowing our way into some inner circle. This new way of seeing not only banishes our loneliness and isolation but makes us compassionate instruments of the kingdom.

REFLECT: What "inner ring" do you yearn to be a part of, and how might you reach out to those who are excluded with you?

DAY 21

Receiving Loneliness

Loneliness comes over us sometimes as a sudden tide. It is one of the terms of our humanness, and, in a sense, therefore, incurable. Yet I have found peace in my loneliest times not only through acceptance of the situation, but through making it an offering to God, who can transfigure it into something for the good of others.

ELISABETH ELLIOT

Now I want you to know, brothers and sisters, that what has happened to me has actually advanced the gospel, so that it has become known throughout the whole imperial guard, and to everyone else, that my imprisonment is because I am in Christ. Most of the brothers have gained confidence in the Lord from my imprisonment and dare even more to speak the word fearlessly. To be sure, some preach Christ out of envy and rivalry, but others out of good will. These preach out of love, knowing that I am appointed for the defense of the gospel;

the others proclaim Christ out of selfish ambition, not sincerely, thinking that they will cause me trouble in my imprisonment. What does it matter? Only that in every way, whether from false motives or true, Christ is proclaimed, and in this I rejoice.

Philippians 1:12–18

Throughout my life and leadership, I have struggled with bouts of loneliness. Sometimes my season of life isolated me, while other times pain was at fault. After decades of being haunted by this terrible ghost, I have learned a very difficult truth: Sometimes we feel lonely because we are truly alone, but sometimes we feel lonely because we *tell* ourselves we are alone.

This is a lesson I learned from both life experience and a longtime study of the apostle Paul. In his letter to the Philippians—easily the most joyful book in all of Scripture—Paul is relentlessly chipper. It is in Philippians that we find some of the most inspirational verses in all of the Bible—verses that are frequently splashed across coffee mugs, sweatshirts, and wall art:

"I can have a peace that transcends all understanding!" (see 4:7).

"I have learned to be content in every situation!" (see 4:11).

"I can do all things through Christ!" (see 4:13).

Had these words been written by any other man, they would have held only half the weight. However, when Paul pens these words, he is under house arrest in Rome. His living conditions are not dire, but they aren't good. All day long, at all times, he is physically tethered to the enemy, a Roman soldier, unsure if he will be released or executed.

To add salt to the wound, a faction of rival Christians is gleefully delighting in his pain. Rather than support Paul in this moment of discouragement and loneliness, these Christians add insult to injury. They gloat. They kick him while he is down.

The ugliness and pettiness of these fellow "Christians" still galls me to this day. Not only is Paul separated from his friends, but he is further alienated by fellow followers of Jesus. I cannot imagine a lonelier moment.

And yet, there is no pity party here. We do not detect a hint of bitterness or despair. Paul misses his friends, yes, but Paul spends no time at all enumerating his sorrows.

His sights are set higher.

Loneliness is another wound that pulls our focus inward, but what makes this struggle especially tricky is that it spirals into a never-ending cycle. Loneliness feeds self-focus, which only feeds more loneliness, because we become unable to see the people around us.

This is a large part of the reason Paul does not succumb to the cycle: His eyes are up. His gaze is on Christ. He is single-minded in his vision, so much so that he is satisfied for others to preach the gospel, even if their motives are mixed.

That said, there is a second reason Paul is not devoured by his own loneliness, which he mentions later on in chapter 4:

> I have learned to be content in whatever circumstances I find myself. I know how to make do with little, and I know how to make do with a lot. In any and all circumstances I have learned the secret of being content—whether well fed or hungry, whether in abundance or in need. I am able to do all things through him who strengthens me. (vv. 11–13)

Paul is articulating a concept that theologian Henri Nouwen describes in his classic book *The Wounded Healer*. In it, Nouwen explains that we are able to come to terms with our loneliness only when we learn to be at home with ourselves, with Christ. Nouwen even goes so far as to call loneliness a *gift*. He explains that we forsake this gift when we "do everything possible to avoid the painful confrontation with our basic human loneliness, and allow ourselves to be trapped by false gods promising immediate satisfaction and quick relief."[1]

Paul is a man who has learned to accept the gift of loneliness. Rather than languish in his isolation, he has learned to be at home with himself and with Christ.

This is the secret to combating the self-centering spiral of loneliness—raising our gaze to Jesus and then making a home with him.

REFLECT: Are there any areas of your life in which you sense Jesus inviting you to make a home with yourself and with him?

DAY 22

Receiving Hiddenness

When they arrived, Samuel saw Eliab and said, "Certainly the LORD's anointed one is here before him."

But the LORD said to Samuel, "Do not look at his appearance or his stature because I have rejected him. Humans do not see what the LORD sees, for humans see what is visible, but the LORD sees the heart."

Jesse called Abinadab and presented him to Samuel. "The LORD hasn't chosen this one either," Samuel said. Then Jesse presented Shammah, but Samuel said, "The LORD hasn't chosen this one either." After Jesse presented seven of his sons to him, Samuel told Jesse, "The LORD hasn't chosen any of these." Samuel asked him, "Are these all the sons you have?"

"There is still the youngest," he answered, "but right now he's tending the sheep." Samuel told Jesse, "Send for him. We won't sit down to eat until he gets here." So Jesse sent for him. He had beautiful eyes and a healthy, handsome appearance.

Then the LORD said, "Anoint him, for he is the one."

1 Samuel 16:6–12

In his book *The Spirit of the Disciplines*, philosopher Dallas Willard lists spiritual practices for cultivating one's faith, and they are—for the most part—exactly what you would expect: prayer, fasting, study, rest. When we think of basic Christian tenets, we tend to think of these.

There is, however, one practice among them that is "not like the others," so to speak, because it seems very un-Christian at first.

That discipline is secrecy.

I will admit to having been surprised the first time I read this one. Aren't Christians supposed to be honest? Transparent? Vulnerable? If anything, secrecy seems like the very reason many of us never fully flourish in Christ.

But Willard is not talking about deception. Instead, he defines secrecy this way: "a continuing relationship with God *independent of the opinions of others*."[1]

The discipline of secrecy is the opposite of image management. Rather than publicly perform good deeds that in turn skew our motives with vanity, the discipline of secrecy nurtures our humility as we obey God for the sake of his attention alone.

The discipline of secrecy is a powerful way to "unbend our souls." And thankfully—or woefully!—we don't have to go looking for it. The opportunity to practice secrecy (or hiddenness) is, for most of us, constantly available.

Feeling unseen is a common human heartache. It's so common, in fact, that the Bible describes many individuals who experience long seasons of hiddenness—Moses,

Joseph, and even Jesus himself—but the person who wrote most prolifically about it was David, in the Psalms.

Although David would one day become the great king of Israel and an ancestor of Christ, his life began in obscurity. In 1 Samuel 16, we catch the first glimpse of his humble beginnings when the prophet Samuel arrives at David's father's home in search of the future king. Jesse, David's father, presents son after son to Samuel, never even suspecting that David is an option.

By the end of this chapter, Samuel anoints David as king, and one would expect his star to finally rise. But that is not what happens. Instead, David remains virtually unknown. At one point, he is even summoned into King Saul's presence—not to lead a charge against the Philistines but to play the lyre. Before David ever faces off with the mighty warrior Goliath, he works as a shepherd and an entertainer.

Of course, he is best known for his first military victories, but what prepared David for leadership and battle was not experience in leadership and battle. What prepared him to be a leader "after [God's] own heart" was humility (1 Sam. 13:14).

Whenever we feel overlooked or unseen, we have two options: We can either thrash against obscurity by trying to make ourselves bigger and more seen. We can chase after notoriety, constantly post online in order to garner validation, and treat our hiddenness as a problem to be fixed.

Or we can receive hiddenness as a gift. We can accept our "shepherd years" as the surest means to refining our impure motives. We can lean into being overlooked and unappreciated, seeing these seasons and situations as sacred invitations into intimacy with Jesus, seeking his approval alone.

How we respond is who we will become. We can become more desperate to center the self, or we can be free.

The choice is ours.

REFLECT: What aspect of your life feels hidden or unseen right now, and what motivations might God be identifying—and possibly purifying—through it?

Receiving Failure

They seized him, led him away, and brought him into the high priest's house. Meanwhile Peter was following at a distance. They lit a fire in the middle of the courtyard and sat down together, and Peter sat among them. When a servant saw him sitting in the light, and looked closely at him, she said, "This man was with him too."

But he denied it: "Woman, I don't know him."

After a little while, someone else saw him and said, "You're one of them too."

"Man, I am not!" Peter said.

About an hour later, another kept insisting, "This man was certainly with him, since he's also a Galilean."

But Peter said, "Man, I don't know what you're talking about!" Immediately, while he was still speaking, a rooster crowed. Then the Lord turned and looked at Peter. So Peter remembered the word of the Lord, how he had said to him, "Before the rooster crows today, you will deny me three times." And he went outside and wept bitterly.

Luke 22:54–62

Have you ever noticed the similarities between Peter and Judas?

Both men were disciples of Jesus, but they had two very different outcomes in life. Judas is infamously remembered as the disciple who betrayed Jesus. He stole from Jesus, conspired against Jesus, and handed him over to the authorities.

And yet, Judas was not the only disciple who betrayed Jesus.

During his final meal with his disciples, Jesus says that not one but two of his disciples will deny him. In addition to Judas, Jesus warns Peter, "Before the rooster crows today, you will deny three times that you know me" (Luke 22:34 NIV). In Matthew's account of this conversation, Peter is adamant that he will *never* do such a thing: "Even if I have to die with you, . . . I will never deny you" (26:35).

Big words.

Unfortunately, Peter did not know himself as well as Jesus did, and shortly after this exchange, he did exactly what he swore he would never do. Not only did he deny Jesus, but he did so without much resistance. Peter folded at the first questioning of a servant girl.

Judas, then, was not the only disciple to betray Jesus. Peter did as well. Both men, both disciples of Jesus who had committed to following him and honoring him with their lives, were unable to do so.

Both Judas *and* Peter failed.

Judging by each of their responses, they understood this. There is nothing quite like the bitter finality of realizing you fell short. Whether you gave it your all and it wasn't enough or it was your character that couldn't go the distance, failure confronts us with a very particular form of shame. The fear that we are not good enough is no longer a theoretical worry. There is now evidence. It has been confirmed.

Humiliation, exclusion, rejection, loneliness, and hiddenness all tempt us toward self-focus but without much direction. We simply languish in the swamp of insecurity, wondering what is wrong with us or how we might prop up the parts of ourselves that feel small.

Failure is different. Failure, or the fear of failure, doesn't make us feel small. In some ways, it makes us feel big. It leads us to believe that our inability, our inadequacy, our ineptitude is too great an obstacle to overcome. Even for God. This is the sort of me-centered script that inhibited Moses and Jeremiah. Moses did not know how to speak (Exod. 4:10). Jeremiah was "only a youth" (Jer. 1:6). Both were terrified of failure, and they were convinced that their shortcomings were big and significant enough to thwart the plans of God.

Judas seemed to think so too. In Matthew 27 Judas realizes what he has done, and he is filled with regret. He returns the money he was paid and pleads on behalf of Jesus, but it's too late. There is nothing to be done. Judas then leaves the religious leaders and takes his own life, believing the terrible lie that his failure was too big an obstacle for the redemption of God.

Peter's story ends differently. Although he fails to be the man, the friend, and the disciple that he vowed to be, and although he is clearly riddled with shame, Peter has seen enough of Jesus to know what he can do with a failure. Unlike Judas, Peter does not let his shame have the final word. Peter does not believe the lie that his failures and flaws are large enough to hinder the grace of God.

Instead, Peter allows his failure to clarify who is the hero of this story. And thankfully, he knows it is not him.

After Jesus's resurrection, Peter becomes a lion of the church. He spreads the gospel far and wide, writes with brilliance and conviction about the meaning of the gospel, and dies a martyr's death. He is, by every measure, not the same man who cowered at the questioning of a young girl.

This is the severe mercy of failure. It rightsizes our expectations of ourselves and clarifies the true meaning of the gospel. It invites us to put down the heavy yoke of self-importance and take up the easy yoke of Christ.

It is also the only real door to grace. Without failure, grace is just a theory.

REFLECT: Failure has a way of becoming the story we tell about ourselves. Are there any failures that shaped you by becoming the story you tell about yourself? Does that story need to be rewritten in light of the gospel?

DAY 24

Receiving Insignificance

How much happier you would be if you only knew that these people care nothing about you! How much larger your life would be if your self could become smaller in it.

G. K. CHESTERTON

"Because the Israelites' cry for help has come to me, and I have also seen the way the Egyptians are oppressing them, therefore, go. I am sending you to Pharaoh so that you may lead my people, the Israelites, out of Egypt."

But Moses asked God, "Who am I that I should go to Pharaoh and that I should bring the Israelites out of Egypt?"

He answered, "I will certainly be with you, and this will be the sign to you that I am the one who sent you: when you bring the people out of Egypt, you will all worship God at this mountain." . . .

But Moses replied to the Lord, "Please, Lord, I have never been eloquent—either in the past or recently or since you have been speaking to your servant—because my mouth and my tongue are sluggish."

The Lord said to him, "Who placed a mouth on humans? Who makes a person mute or deaf, seeing or blind? Is it not I, the Lord? Now go! I will help you speak and I will teach you what to say."

Moses said, "Please, Lord, send someone else."

Exodus 3:9–12; 4:10–13

There is a paradox that sits at the center of the Christian faith: As people made in the image of God, each of us possesses eternal value. We are marvelous and wonderful, and divine echoes of our heavenly Creator reverberate throughout our entire beings.

Also, we don't matter nearly as much as we think we do.

Depending on the day, we need to be reminded of one or the other of those two truths. For those of us who grew up in a home where lies about our worth were spoken over us, or who were used and abused in romantic relationships, we need the first truth especially and repeatedly. We need to be reminded of our inherent, God-given goodness.

But sometimes, we need to be reminded of our insignificance and smallness, because this can be freeing too.

This is exactly the sort of reminder Moses needs in Exodus 3 and 4. God has just appeared to Moses in a burning bush and has instructed him to go to Pharaoh and deliver his people. Moses, however, thinks this is a terrible idea. He raises objection after objection. "What if Pharaoh doesn't listen? How will they know?" As Moses brings excuse after excuse about why he is not cut out for this job, God does not respond with encouragement or coddling. He does not soothe Moses's anxieties by reassuring him of his potential. When Moses pleads with God, saying, "I cannot do this, I am not able," God essentially agrees.

"Yes, that's exactly right. Of course you cannot do this. You were never going to do this. Who invented mouths? Who invented speech? Who created ears to hear and minds to understand? Was it not I? I am the one who will do this, so do not be afraid, and follow me" (see Exod. 4:11).

Moses's mistake was overestimating his own significance. He thought he was the hero of the story, a misunderstanding that saddled him with unbearable pressure. What empowered Moses was not remembering how talented or experienced or special he was but, as author Jen Wilkin once put it, "changing the subject."[1] He remembered it was God who was able, not him.

Anytime we overestimate our significance, anytime we make the mistake of thinking we are bigger than we are, we trigger insecurity. That is also the counterintuitive freedom of remembering it's not about you.

When your friend never texted back? *That was not about you.*

When your spouse exploded on you in the kitchen? *That was not about you.*

When the server was rude despite your best attempts to be kind? *That was not about you.*

When that friend at church seemed uninterested in talking to you? *That was not about you.*

When your parents divorced? *That was not about you.*

When your parent couldn't stop drinking? *That was not about you.*

When your adult child made an irresponsible decision? *That was not about you.*

When God calls you to something far beyond your capacity? *Ultimately, it's not about you.* The outcome does not rise and fall on you.

Each of us is a precious, treasured, beloved child of God. But we are not the center of the story he is writing.

This, strangely, is good news.

REFLECT: When was the last time you made something about you that was probably not about you? How might you have processed the experience differently if you had remembered that you were not the center of the story?

Receiving Mediocrity

> Make it your ambition to lead a quiet life: You should mind your own business and work with your hands, just as we told you, so that your daily life may win the respect of outsiders and so that you will not be dependent on anybody.
>
> 1 Thessalonians 4:11–12 NIV

Sometimes God puts to death our vanity and our pride, not through breathtaking humiliations or gut-wrenching rejections, but through the gnawing ache of being ordinary.

This is a discomfort I became very familiar with through the process of starting a church. In its earliest stages, a young church is almost entirely volunteer-led, which means every leader is also working another full-time job, and the risk of overwhelm is extremely high. Young churches are notorious for burning through volunteers. We did not want that to be our story, so we chose the health of our people over the quality of our production.

It sounds noble on paper, and to some extent it was, but it was also extremely messy. Practically speaking, prioritizing people over production meant looking unpolished and even unprofessional at times. Sometimes we didn't have enough instrumentalists for a full worship team because we didn't want volunteers playing every Sunday. Sometimes the sound or lighting was off because we couldn't afford to hire someone to oversee production. Then there were the mornings when all of our equipment simply stopped working. I will never forget the Sunday when we had to make a game-day, executive decision not to have music and to skip straight to the sermon because so many things had gone wrong.

These experiences were humbling, to say the least. Whenever new people were visiting on those "off" Sundays, I wanted to hunt them down and explain everything. "We aren't normally this disorganized! A bunch of things went wrong. Also, we see the problems. We know where we could do better! We are simply choosing the health of our leaders."

Unfortunately, I could not do that, and it made me anxious and stressed-out whenever I tried.

Eventually, I chose humility instead. I chose to receive the appearance of mediocrity because I knew our values were in line with Christ's, and at the end of the day, our call was not to put on a good show but to shepherd people—which we can do without a full band on Sunday morning.

Not everyone can relate to this particular struggle, but we can all relate to the sting of mediocrity. We feel it when we hold our tongues in humility, or practice patience, only to have this gesture interpreted as incompetence. We experience it when we choose not to work one hundred hours a week to get ahead at our job, because our priority is our family. Or perhaps most painfully of all, we feel it when we have worked as hard as we possibly can—poured everything we have into a dream—to experience only marginal success.

These moments, when we must accept the appearance of mediocrity—or worse, the reality of it—seem so insignificant in comparison to the anguish of failure or rejection, but they can be just as agonizing. This is because mediocrity is often accompanied by public humiliation or the death of a dream. We are forced to reckon with the versions of ourselves we hoped to be, or the life we hoped to attain, versus the ones we actually are. Whether we choose ordinariness for a reason, or it is thrust upon us, the experience lays immediate claim to our pride.

And pride puts up a good fight.

That battle, however, is ultimately what led me to surrender my need to be impressive or appear put together. At some point I realized it simply wasn't worth it. It was too exhausting. The emotional energy I was investing in my image was not paying dividends back into my soul.

In contrast, there is freedom in accepting the assignment God has given us and being satisfied with stewarding it faithfully. That does not mean the quality of our work doesn't matter or that we should settle for lower standards.

It does mean our highest value must never be what other people think or some other worldly metric of success. In the kingdom of God, our metric is always "What kind of person am I becoming?" We should ask, "Am I becoming more like Jesus, or less? Am I becoming a spouse, a parent, a pastor, a friend who lives more like Jesus, or less?"

Sometimes we must receive the world's standard of mediocrity to choose the better thing.

The good news is this: It is possible to live an ordinary life that is extraordinary in the kingdom of God. We won't always see the fruit of our choices now, but one day, we most assuredly will.

REFLECT: Is there an area of your life in which you are driven by the desire to be accomplished or exceptional? How has that desire affected your mental health or your relationships?

Self-Denial
and Body Image

> Don't you know that your body is a temple of the Holy
> Spirit who is in you, whom you have from God? You are
> not your own, for you were bought at a price. So glorify
> God with your body.
>
> 1 Corinthians 6:19–20

One of the most surprising truths about self-denial is that it does not require a rejection of the body. Quite the opposite, in fact. At some time or another, denying ourselves will actually mean *receiving* our bodies. Making peace with our bodies as they are will be the very mechanism by which we resist the idolatry of the self.

This is a truth I learned only in adulthood. For a long time, I thought I had a fantastic relationship with my body. I did not struggle with insecurity or excessive vanity. I did not hate my body, and I did not think too much about it either.

In retrospect, this "healthy" relationship was actually quite conditional. Part of the reason I had a good relationship with my body was because my body was cooperating with me. I was young. I was healthy. I had not yet started having children. I could, more or less, control my body.

It was not until my body stopped submitting to me that my true relationship with my appearance was revealed. Once my hips were stretched by children, my back began to ache with age, and wrinkles began to form across my neck and forehead, I started thinking about my body and my appearance very differently.

What I did not realize until then is that I had only approved of my body because it had served my self-image; it participated in my idolatry of self. But when it was no longer able to perform this duty, I developed a new, adversarial relationship with my body image.

Sooner or later we all reach this point—when our bodies fail to cooperate. Whether it is tied to our appearance or our health, our self-esteem begins to wobble if any part of it depends on our bodies. And when this happens, we have a choice: to resist our bodies or to receive them.

When we receive our bodies with all their imperfections, aches, and pains, we—ironically—starve the "flesh." In the New Testament, the "flesh" is not a synonym for the body but instead refers to sinful human nature. It is the part of us that would rather depend on the self than on God. Our bodies will one day be resurrected, and our flesh will ultimately be put to death; this is a spiritual process we can begin participating in now by embracing the weaknesses of our bodies so that God's power might be made perfect in us.

Receiving our bodies is also an invitation to center others instead of ourselves. When we fight the decline of our bodies as if our satisfaction depends on it, that becomes the "gospel" we preach to everyone around us. But when we resist our economy of appearance by receiving our bodies with all their weaknesses and imperfections, we challenge the idols of youth and beauty that keep so many of our neighbors in bondage.

This is, after all, what Jesus did. Philippians 2:6–8 tells us Jesus denied himself glory and lowered himself. He quite literally received a human body and humbled his appearance as an act of love for us.

We can do the same. Whenever we are confronted by bodily challenges or imperfections, God invites us to reconsider our relationship with our bodies. Will we continue to make our bodies about us? Or will we recognize these moments as an opportunity to resist our image-obsessed culture of comparison by receiving and delighting in the bodies we have?

To be clear, there is absolutely nothing wrong with staying fit or eating healthy or enjoying makeup or fashion. God commands us to care for and enjoy creation, and that includes stewarding the health of our bodies. Makeup and fashion can be a form of creativity and play. But on the days when our bodily imperfections are showing, or we cannot conceal the signs of age, we are invited to surrender to a higher good. When we receive our bodies as they are, rather than resist them, we restore them to their created purpose: to serve as vessels of God's love.

REFLECT: Take a moment to pause and listen to the Holy Spirit. How is he inviting you to receive your body right now?

Denying Yourself without Neglecting Yourself

Sacrifice is a delicate balance of selflessness and self-respect.

ALISON COOK

Then God said, "Let us make man in our image, according to our likeness. They will rule the fish of the sea, the birds of the sky, the livestock, the whole earth, and the creatures that crawl on the earth."

> So God created man
> in his own image;
> he created him in the image of God;
> he created them male and female.

God blessed them, and God said to them, "Be fruitful, multiply, fill the earth, and subdue it. Rule the fish of the sea, the birds of the sky, and every creature that crawls on the earth." God also said, "Look, I have given you every seed-bearing plant on the surface of the entire earth and every tree whose fruit contains seed. This will be food for you, for all the wildlife of the earth, for every bird of the sky, and for every creature that crawls on the earth—everything having the breath of life in it—I have given every green plant for food." And it was so. God saw all that he had made, and it was very good indeed.

Genesis 1:26–31

W hat is the difference between self-denial and self-neglect?
It would be reckless not to address this question, since Jesus's teachings on the matter have often been twisted to mean something he never intended (see Matt. 16:24). Some victims of abuse, for example, have interpreted his words to mean they must remain in their abuse. In countless situations, Christians have wrung themselves out mentally, physically, and spiritually, serving their churches or their families in the name of "laying themselves down."

This mistake is, to some extent, understandable. There is a cross at the center of our gospel, after all. A cross that Jesus invites his followers to take up. Pain, suffering, and self-sacrifice are guarantees of the Christian life.

And yet there is a critical difference between self-denial and self-neglect. One operates out of a whole and healed sense of self, and the other does not. Healthy self-denial recognizes the goodness of the self and seeks to guard it against the trappings of the flesh. It also desires to train the self in godliness, not as a form of punishment but as an act of self-love.

Self-neglect is something else. It is a kind of self-abandonment in which we engage in self-sacrifice and self-sabotage because we do not actually value ourselves. This behavior can appear extremely noble and self-giving but actually derives from a low view of and value for ourselves.

In other cases (and sometimes these cases overlap), self-neglect occurs when we are seeking to validate ourselves, or find our identity, in sources other than God. For instance, a mother might neglect her sleep, diet, and mental health, all in service to her family because her identity is so bound up in being a caregiver. A pastor might be the chief of servants—always the first to show up, always the last to leave, always available to the people in his church—not because he is a saint but because his identity is overly tied to his work.

These temptations underscore the importance of affirming the self before denying the self. Both self-neglect and self-abandonment are rooted in bad theology, one that does not take seriously the creation narrative of Genesis 1. In the very first chapter of the Bible, God calls the human creation "good," and this goodness is not erased by sin; it is inherent to our being.

Furthermore, God commissions humanity to "subdue" the earth (v. 28), a command that is clarified in chapter 2, when God instructs Adam to "work it and watch over it" (v. 15). God is not unleashing Adam to control creation but to tend it.

And we are a part of that creation.

Our bodies, our minds, our entire beings are all a part of the goodness of creation. And, as descendants of Adam, we are charged with "watching over" ourselves with as much wisdom and urgency as any other part of God's created world. We do this because we belong to God, not to ourselves. We are merely caretakers.

It is both biblical and right to value what God values, and Scripture tells us that God calls each one of us good. Self-neglect is out of step with this theological truth, because God expects us to take good care of his good things.

REFLECT: Is self-neglect a temptation you experience? If so, take some time to examine what priorities, beliefs, or fears are behind it.

Movement 4

———

TURNING TOWARD GOD

The Firstfruits
of Your Attention

You become what you give your attention to.

EPICTETUS

> Keep this Book of the Law always on your lips; meditate
> on it day and night, so that you may be careful to do
> everything written in it. Then you will be prosperous
> and successful.
>
> Joshua 1:8 NIV

Throughout the Old Testament, Scripture exhorts God's people to meditate on God's Law as often as we can. We are instructed to study it day and night. To write it on our doorposts. To tie it around our hands and bind it to our foreheads (Deut. 6:8). The language of this practice is both straightforward and consistent, but I will confess I have always interpreted it figuratively. "Study Scripture dutifully and rigorously," I assumed it was emphasizing.

However, the Jewish people have not, historically, interpreted these passages figuratively at all. They have quite literally done these things. During Jesus's time, the religious leaders were known to don "phylacteries" (Matt. 23:5)—small leather boxes containing Hebrew texts—on their foreheads. Similarly, the mezuzah is a small piece of parchment containing Hebrew Scripture that is placed on the doorposts of Jewish homes.

One reason I have always read these passages figuratively is that I long misunderstood what was meant by "the Law." For God's people, this term is shorthand for the first five books of the Old Testament, also known as the Torah. Meditating on God's Law does not mean we memorize a bunch of rules but soak in God's inspired words to his people. One could also argue that the spirit of these verses is not limited to the first five books of the Bible but includes the whole of Scripture.

That was my first misunderstanding. My second misunderstanding was related to *why* we might do this. Why would God want us to meditate on his Word so constantly? Was this simply a way for us to become nice, law-abiding Christian people?

Not exactly.

Instead, these commands have more to do with the ancient wisdom of Epictetus, who observed that what we give our attention to is what we will become. What we focus on is what forms us, which is a sobering reminder in the age of smartphones and social media. Now more than ever, we belong to an attention economy, in which corporations are constantly competing for our attention. And unfortunately, so are our children. Focus is an increasingly rare and valuable resource, because out of it flows the direction and priorities of our lives.

And *this*, this is why God asks us to give the firstfruits of our attention to him. He will not compete for our attention, but he makes no bones about the importance of it. What we give our attention to either expands our souls or shrinks them.

Meditating on God's Law is not an item to be checked off the Christian checklist. It is not one more thing to add to your day, and it has nothing to do with "being good." Instead, meditating on Scripture is how we steward the momentum of our souls.

REFLECT: Meditating on Scripture does not have to look like a "quiet time" in the morning. We can read God's Word during the day. We can listen to it being read to us, or we can utilize a resource to guide us through it, such as a study book or an app. What works best to help you meditate on God's Word? Do you need to make a change in how you engage with Scripture?

Why We Worship

In worship we don't just come to show God our devotion and give him our praise; we are called to worship because in this encounter God (re)makes and molds us top-down. Worship is the arena in which God recalibrates our hearts, reforms our desires, and rehabituates our loves. Worship isn't just something we do; it is where God does something to us. Worship is the heart of discipleship because it is the gymnasium in which God retrains our hearts.

JAMES K. A. SMITH

The LORD is great and is highly praised;
his greatness is unsearchable. . . .

The LORD is gracious and compassionate,
slow to anger and great in faithful love.
The LORD is good to everyone;
his compassion rests on all he has made. . . .

> The LORD is righteous in all his ways
> and faithful in all his acts.
>
> Psalm 145:3, 8–9, 17

"You need to stop the train."
This was the advice my counselor gave me one afternoon as I described the spiraling thoughts of my insecurities. The thoughts were so powerful and repetitive that I became convinced they were true. These me-centered scripts were hijacking my peace and contentment, and I wanted to make them stop, which is what prompted my counselor to make this statement: "These scripts in your brain are a train of thought that needs to be disrupted. You need to stop the train."

But the question was *how?*

It would be so much easier if we could simply turn off our negative thoughts like a faucet, but our minds do not work that way. We need something to turn our attention *to*, and figuring that out led to the greatest liberation of my life, second only to meeting Jesus.

What I discovered in my journey toward stopping the train—and more importantly, to breaking the hold my insecurities had on me—is that the best way to disrupt those trains of thought and me-centered scripts is through worship. More precisely, by meditating on and praising the character and ways of God. Worship, I discovered, is what liberates the self from the bondage of self-preoccupation.

The bondage-breaking power of worship is why so many of the Psalms extol the character and faithfulness of God. David wrote some of his most poignant and memorable psalms of praise when fleeing for his life, not while reveling in the lap of luxury. The Psalms were not written out of the overflow of seasons of comfort and prosperity, but they were instead his means of survival. Worship was his lifeline. Had David spent too long meditating on Saul's hate instead of God's love, or meditating on his loneliness instead of God's nearness, he may have been tempted to despair. And at times he was.

But the freedom-fighting power of worship is why so many of the darkest psalms end in praise. Not because David necessarily felt joyful or thankful or full of awe but because God's character was his refuge and his hope.

God invites us to worship for many reasons: It is how we reorient ourselves to reality, and it is also how we enjoy him. But God also invites us to worship him because it is for our good. When our thoughts are spiraling with me-centered lies or assumptions that keep us locked in insecurity and pain, we need to stop the train, and worship has the power to do that. Why? Because worship is not merely a distraction from what ails us; it is what we were created to do. When we wrench our focus off of ourselves and our circumstances and look to the goodness of God—whether that is through singing worship songs on Sunday morning or in the car on a Tuesday afternoon, making time to revel in his marvelous creation, or meditating on his character throughout the day—we are returning to our soul's home base.

While there are plenty of studies about the effectiveness of disrupting our toxic patterns of thought—and worship accomplishes this too—it is also more than a mental hack. Worship is the purest expression of our soul's intended design, which is why it does more than simply stop the train. Worship sets us free.

> **REFLECT:** Read Psalm 145 in its entirety. What parts of this psalm do you find most comforting? Write down any statements that can help you "stop the train" of your insecurities and refocus on the goodness of God.

DAY 30

Look Ahead

Self-seeking is the gate by which a soul departs from peace;
and total abandonment to the will of God, that by which
it returns.

JEANNE GUYON

> Let your eyes look forward;
> fix your gaze straight ahead.
> Carefully consider the path for your feet,
> and all your ways will be established.
> Don't turn to the right or to the left;
> keep your feet away from evil.
>
> Proverbs 4:25–27

When my husband and I first planted our church together, I was constantly distracted by what other churches were doing and compared our

151

church to theirs. From our website to our vision statement to the way we welcomed visitors, I second-guessed everything. We would formulate a plan, pray over it, and feel confident about it, only to reassess it when we discovered another church "doing it better."

A year or two into this process, I began to realize what was really happening inside me every time we compared ourselves to another church. I imagined myself driving down a highway toward a specific destination only to notice a billboard advertising a better destination. Each time I saw one of these billboards, I rubbernecked to the point of slowing down and swerving or I exited the highway entirely. Each billboard either distracted or derailed me from the destination God had appointed me to pursue.

We all experience the same derailing effect when we go for a run. If we look to the side or if we stare too long at some far-off point of interest—basically, if we look anywhere but straight ahead—our gait will begin to wobble. This is how countless runners (and walkers) have collided with telephone poles; they were looking at their phones instead of where they were going.

This is the danger of comparison. It is not simply that it steals our joy and contentment but that it is a distraction. Comparison takes our eyes off the work, or the life, to which we have been called, leaving us unable to steward God's work faithfully. That is why focus matters. Hebrews 12 says that in the "race of faith," if we take our eyes off of Jesus for too long and compare ourselves to others, we will start running toward others instead, often with disastrous consequences. The passage uses this same language, urging us to "run with endurance the race that lies before us, keeping our eyes on Jesus" (vv. 1–2). Likewise in Proverbs 4:27, we are warned not to "turn to the right or to the left." If we focus on anything other than Christ, we risk ending up somewhere else entirely.

Of course, not all "road signs" are bad. Some tell us how to arrive at our destination more safely. Others tell us how to navigate bends in the road or perilous weather conditions. This sort of "looking" is not a distraction, but wisdom. My husband and I are wise to learn from other churches. Runners are wise to observe the street-crossing lights. All of us would be wise to listen to counsel from other believers on how to follow Jesus well.

But on the path to self-forgetfulness, there can be only one true *focus*. Jesus is not just another helper on the journey but the destination itself.

REFLECT: What "road signs" in your life threaten to derail your focus? What are you tempted to run toward (perhaps it is a vain thing; perhaps it is a good thing) instead of running toward Christ?

Look Up

The mind feasts on what it focuses on. What consumes my thinking will be the making or the breaking of my identity.

LYSA TERKEURST

Jesus came toward them walking on the sea very early in the morning. When the disciples saw him walking on the sea, they were terrified. "It's a ghost!" they said, and they cried out in fear.

Immediately Jesus spoke to them. "Have courage! It is I. Don't be afraid."

"Lord, if it's you," Peter answered him, "command me to come to you on the water."

He said, "Come."

And climbing out of the boat, Peter started walking on the water and came toward Jesus. But when he saw the strength of the wind, he was afraid, and beginning to sink he cried out, "Lord, save me!"

Immediately Jesus reached out his hand, caught hold of him, and said to him, "You of little faith, why did you doubt?"

Matthew 14:25–31

Recently I had a humbling realization about my past. When I was in my twenties, I experienced a long stretch of relationship wounds that haunted me for years. During that season, I went through romantic breakups and friendship breakups that left me feeling broken and insecure. I felt rejected and left out and very alone. This period of my life was so painful that it overshadowed my memory of the entire decade. Whenever I would describe my twenties to people, I would often say it was the worst decade of my life.

In many ways, it was.

Except that it wasn't the whole decade; it was only four years.

I met my husband, Ike, in my midtwenties, and the rest of that decade was wonderful. The tumultuous part was actually relatively short in comparison, but I had inflated its duration in my memory. In truth, that stormy season of my life did not last a decade, or even half of one.

I was stunned when I realized what a short period of time that season actually represented. Then again, focus has that effect. When we focus on things in our lives—good or bad— they become outsized in our imaginations. This is true of our circumstances, and it is also true of self-preoccupation. Focus amplifies.

When we place ourselves at the center of a story, especially a painful one, everything becomes heightened, and this is exactly the trap that Peter fell into in Matthew 14.

In this well-known story, Peter climbs out of the boat to join Jesus in the water. Miraculously, Peter is able to take a few steps until he decides to look down. Once his focus shifts off of Jesus and onto the waves, his courage falters.

This story serves as a powerful reminder to guard our focus when the waves of our circumstances, our emotions, or our me-centered thoughts loom large. As soon as our focus begins to drift off of Jesus, our peace and security will drift with it. What will seem "big" to us is not the omnipotence and omniscience of God, but the storm around us—or inside of us.

This is also the essence of worship, in which we raise our gaze off of the waves and onto the One who commands them. When we worship, we exercise agency over our focus by choosing what to amplify.

If you find yourself in a stormy season of life, or assaulted by relentless, me-centered fears, the lesson of Matthew 14 is simple: look up.

REFLECT: What storm feels "big" to you right now? Where do you sense Jesus in the midst of this storm?

Look Back

Samuel was offering the burnt offering as the Philistines approached to fight against Israel. The LORD thundered loudly against the Philistines that day and threw them into such confusion that they were defeated by Israel. Then the men of Israel charged out of Mizpah and pursued the Philistines striking them down all the way to a place below Beth-car.

Afterward, Samuel took a stone and set it upright between Mizpah and Shen. He named it Ebenezer, explaining, "The LORD has helped us to this point."

1 Samuel 7:10–12

W ho is looking out for *me?*"
Without my realizing it, this question has driven some of my most self-oriented actions. The fear that if I didn't speak up for myself, no one would.

The concern that if I didn't tout my accomplishments, no one would. If I didn't keep all of my money—instead of being generous with it—I wouldn't have enough. If I didn't manipulate my way into being included, I would be left out. If I didn't post on social media about how upset I was, nobody would reach out.

These narratives are very often understandable. For anyone who grew up in a dysfunctional home or who experienced a season of life when their physical or emotional needs went unmet, this fear would run deep. And yet that is not my story. I did not grow up with any sort of want. My childhood home was safe and secure and full of love. So why did I wrestle with the survival narrative that I needed to look out for me? That no one was going to do a better job of taking care of me than *me*?

The reason we all experience scarcity thinking, regardless of our backgrounds, is that it is not ultimately rooted in our stories. It's rooted in sin. Adam and Eve acted on the fear that God was holding out on them in Genesis 3, and we have been reenacting that moment ever since. Of course, our life experience can give credence to this fear, but it doesn't have to. As long as we are humans on this earth, we will find ourselves tempted by the same lie as our original parents.

When we fall prey to this thinking, there is one inevitable consequence: dragging our focus selfward. Scarcity has that effect, which is why we must actively resist it, and when we look to Scripture for examples of how to do this, there is a very obvious theme.

In order to stave off their fears about the future, the Israelites oriented their entire calendars around the discipline of remembering. From the way they planned their festivals to their feasts, the Israelites understood that God's faithfulness in the past was their reassurance for the future. This practice of remembering is also why, in 1 Samuel 7:12, Samuel created an Ebenezer of God's faithfulness, a word that literally means "stone of help." Whenever future generations of Israelites would see this rock, they would remember God's protection and deliverance in the past, and it would serve as its own sort of protection against the survival mentality that starves the imagination with self-oriented fear.

The same is true today.

Whenever we notice our thoughts spiraling with anxieties about provision, recognition, or the threat of destruction, God's faithfulness in the past can deliver us from the false gospel of self-preservation. This powerful practice of remembering is why, every week, Christians around the world gather and take communion together. When we eat the bread and drink from the cup, we remember the heights and depths and lengths that God has gone to, to restore us back to ourselves and back to him. If God is for us, then no one can be against us—a truth cemented by the cross. Because of Jesus's great love for us, we can entrust ourselves to him, knowing our lives will be infinitely safer in his hands than our own.

REFLECT: How has God been faithful to you in the past? Consider an "Ebenezer" you might create to mark and remember God's faithfulness to you.

DAY 33

Look to Scripture

> Then Jesus was led up by the Spirit into the wilderness to be tempted by the devil. After he had fasted forty days and forty nights, he was hungry. Then the tempter approached him and said, "If you are the Son of God, tell these stones to become bread."
>
> He answered, "It is written: Man must not live on bread alone but on every word that comes from the mouth of God."
>
> Matthew 4:1–4

You are not the center of your story. But the enemy would love for you to think that you are.

This has, in fact, always been Satan's tactic. Since the beginning, he has understood our great appetite for stories about ourselves. Take Adam and Eve. In Genesis 3, Satan approaches the first man and woman with promises of knowledge, power, glory, and control. Although they have been thriving in an environment centered on God and his goodness, Satan offers them the opportunity to tell a new story, one more focused on themselves.

Adam and Eve are so enticed by this offer that they swallow it whole—both literally and figuratively—and sadly, we have been falling for the same scam ever since. Whether Satan is feeding our ego with promises of power and glory or shaming us with lies about our abilities or worth, we are always inclined to believe versions of the truth that center around us.

Unsurprisingly, this focus has never served us well. Whenever we center ourselves—whether through vanity, self-pity, or even insecure self-preoccupation—we reenact the fall and its consequences, over and over.

What, then, is the answer? How do we break this cycle? How do we guard ourselves against our own predisposition to believe lies and half-truths about ourselves?

Enter Jesus.

In Matthew 4, Satan tempts Jesus using the exact same game plan he once used against Adam and Eve: offers of power, glory, status. This scene is, in many ways, a reenactment of Genesis 3, but with one critical difference: Jesus does not believe the devil's lies, nor is he enticed by the devil's narcissistic promises. Instead, Jesus does what Adam and Eve were not able to do: He combats the devil's lies with God's truth.

More specifically, he quotes Scripture:

> "Man must not live on bread alone but on every word
> that comes from the mouth of God" (v. 4).
> "Do not test the Lord your God" (v. 7).
> "Worship the Lord your God, and serve only him"
> (v. 10).

Jesus Christ—God made flesh—does not respond with spontaneous revelation. He does not speak fresh and newly inspired words of God. Instead, he does something that any one of his followers has the power to do: He responds to the lies of the devil with the truth of Scripture.

In doing so, Jesus hands us a new legacy. No longer are we doomed to reenact Adam and Eve's failures. Now, whenever we face the temptation to center ourselves—either arrogantly or out of insecurity—we know that God has left us equipped. Not only has he sent his Holy Spirit to empower us with wisdom, but he has given us his Word to guard us. When we meditate on Scripture and arm ourselves with it, we stand ready to combat the enemy's lies, just as Jesus once did.

So arm yourself. Get ready now. You cannot identify Satan's lies if you do not know the truth. Nor can you defend yourself against the attacks of the enemy without the sword of the Spirit, God's Word. This is why we are instructed to spend time in Scripture every day. Not because it is what "good Christians" do, and not because it is the only way to please God. We are invited to meditate on God's Word day and night because the enemy tells a good story, but our Father in heaven tells a better one.

REFLECT: Identify any me-centered lies that the enemy is tempting you with right now. What passages of Scripture are a truthful weapon to wield in response?

DAY 34

Look for Beauty

To bear witness to the beautiful is not to be conflated with escapism or naivete. It is a deep form of survival inherited from our ancestors. In a time when we have more access than ever before to the traumas of this world, how will you resist the tide of despair? Let beauty be your anchor.

COLE ARTHUR RILEY

Finally brothers and sisters, whatever is true, whatever is honorable, whatever is just, whatever is pure, whatever is lovely, whatever is commendable—if there is any moral excellence and if there is anything praiseworthy—dwell on these things.

Philippians 4:8

L ast summer, in celebration of Ike's and my anniversary, we flew out to Utah to visit Zion National Park. If you have never seen this canyon, its colors and contours truly defy description. They are otherworldly. While there, we hiked Zion's most famous trail, The Narrows, which is a slender passage carved out by the river. This feature is what makes the hike so unique; the entire path is *in* the water. As we snaked our way through its tight bends and curves, every turn revealed a new and breathtaking view. The walls stretched toward the sky in soft waves, each displaying bands of orange, brown, and red as if they had been painted by hand.

Even the mouth of the canyon, where our hotel was located, was surrounded by soaring rust-colored peaks. Every time we stepped outside, I gasped and staggered backwards, as if I were seeing the mountains for the first time. My brain simply could not store the true majesty and beauty of the scenery into my working memory. It is difficult to describe, capture, or remember in its fullness.

Multiple times throughout our stay there, I commented to Ike that God is quite clearly an artist. In some places, the pigment of the rock was textured by erosion and had the appearance of actual brushstrokes. One could almost imagine God stooping down and carefully selecting the right colors before applying each tone in just the right way. It was impossible to behold this beauty without remembering the One who created it, which is to say, it was impossible to behold this beauty without worshiping.

This is the inherent nature of beauty: to draw us outside of ourselves and point to its Originator. And this aspect of beauty is not limited to the wonders of creation but applies to beauty in all its many forms. We experience the same sort of transcendence when we view a sublime piece of art, read an inspired work of literature, or listen to music so heavenly it makes us weep. We can also experience the awe of beauty in the mundane moments of our lives. I regularly marvel at the beauty of my daughter or the way the afternoon light streams in through our back porch screen. When we take time to notice beauty, it expands the margins of our vision and thus our mindsets. It broadens our horizons by resituating us in the expansive world around us, reminding us how relatively small we are.

This is the reason why many people feel closest to God in nature, and while nature is no substitute for knowing God through Christ, it provides us a glorious taste of his goodness. When we behold nature—or any other beauty in the world—it is not an exaggeration to say we are meditating on what God is like.

As a leader in ministry, I have learned the importance of beholding beauty in order to guard my vision and sustain my soul. It is tempting to allow the traumas and challenges of leadership to become my whole vision, dragging my focus down into the mire. Beauty, however, raises my gaze. When I take time to notice the ocean blue of my son's eyes, to study the icons in our church offices, or to listen to a composer who somehow captures joy and melancholy all in the same note, my soul unfurls.

Make time for beauty. Look for it. Throughout your day, notice it where you can. Pause to savor it. Delight in it. Thank God for it. And remember that all beauty, no matter where you find it, is pointing ahead to the kingdom.

REFLECT: What is your favorite way to experience beauty? If this is not already a regular part of your day, how might you incorporate it?

Look for Laughter

Laughter is the closest thing to the grace of God.

KARL BARTH

> When the LORD restored the fortunes of Zion,
> we were like those who dream.
> Our mouths were filled with laughter then,
> and our tongues with shouts of joy.
> Then they said among the nations,
> "The LORD has done great things for them."
> The LORD had done great things for us;
> we were joyful.
>
> Psalm 126:1–3

God invented laughter. I tell my kids this regularly, not only because it is true but because too many Christians do not seem to understand it. Followers of Jesus can take themselves very seriously. This is not true of every Christian or every church, but we can be a rather stuffy bunch! Not to mention the humorless self-importance of social media bickering. In these contentious environments, there is an implicit assumption that faith is a solemn affair. And at times it can be. But God is also the God of laughter, humor, and fun. He did, after all, create the duck-billed platypus and farts. Fun and silliness are not less spiritual activities but are heavenly in a very real sense.

This is the very reason laughter draws us out of ourselves.

Maybe you have had this experience: You are home, isolated, lonely, feeling rejected, misunderstood, or insecure, and then a friend sends you a funny text, and the anguish dissipates just a bit. Or maybe you go to a dinner you had already planned but are no longer in the mood to attend, and by the end of the meal you are laughing until you cry.

Laughter draws us out of our isolation and self-pity, because God designed it to.

In fact, scientific studies have proven this to be true. According to the Mayo Clinic, laughter grants us all sorts of physical and mental benefits. It reduces stress, soothes tension, improves the function of our immune system, and can even relieve pain.[1] When Proverbs 17:22 says that a "joyful heart is good medicine," it is quite literally true.

Laughter is also a simple and delightful way to disrupt our me-centered spiraling. In his book *Managing Leadership Anxiety*, author Steve Cuss writes that one sign of anxiety is "a lack of playfulness and laughter and an overabundance of earnestness."[2] When we take ourselves too seriously or descend into defeatism or become paralyzed by me-centered fears, we are not thinking clearly because anxiety and insecurity are in the driver's seat.

One way to de-escalate anxiety, Cuss writes, is to develop a "knack for playfulness."[3] When we are able to laugh—especially with others—we are drawn outside of ourselves to revel in what theologian Karl Barth describes as a true "grace of God."[4]

Friendship is without a doubt one of the most delightful sources of laughter, but don't stop there. Whether it is a movie, a TV show, an author, your children, or an online video of screaming goats, pay attention to what makes you laugh, because laughter has the potential to elevate your soul. Not all laughter is created equal, of course (mean laughter or crass laughter, for example), but as we seek to raise our gaze, we do ourselves a disservice if we assume life must be a somber affair. One of the most marvelous yet most forgotten truths about God is that he created us to laugh. Just as he does.

REFLECT: What is one way you can cultivate more laughter in your life? Who are the fun and playful people you can reach out to when your me-centered thoughts are spiraling?

Movement 5

———

TURNING
TOWARD
OTHERS

Love Your Neighbor

Loving someone liberates the lover as well as the beloved.

MAYA ANGELOU

"Teacher, which command in the law is the greatest?"
He said to him, "Love the Lord your God with all your heart, with all your soul, and with all your mind. This is the greatest and most important command. The second is like it: Love your neighbor as yourself. All the Law and the Prophets depend on these two commands."

Matthew 22:36–40

This is going to sound strange, but one of my favorite things to do for young people in our church is help them navigate a breakup.
I am not an expert at many things, but this I can speak to! My twenties were so checkered with horrible relationship

endings that I not only understand the devastation personally but have done the work to help others process it too. Every time my husband and I sit with a young man or young woman as they sob on the couch in our church offices, I feel more than prepared to handle their grief. As Mordecai once declared in the book of Esther, I was forged in the fire of breakups "for such a time as this!"

Having said that, the real reason I love these meetings is that they give me a sense of meaning. They feel redemptive. Every time I walk beside another person through a romantic breakup, I am reminded that my pain was not in vain. Though I am long past grieving old relationship endings, there is still a sense in which ministering to others also ministers to me. Fifteen years after my husband and I said "I do," these conversations continue to yield new insights into myself and my own journey.

To put it another way, helping others also helps me.

That is the power of giving purpose to our pain. When our own story becomes the birthplace of mission, it contributes not only to the healing of others but to our own healing as well.

Most of us know this intuitively, of course, which is why countless organizations are organized around this principle. Alcoholics Anonymous, for example, is probably best known for its Twelve Step program, but that is not the secret of its success. The founder of AA was a man named Bill Wilson, and although Bill's conversion to Christianity played a significant role in his sobriety, Bill's biographer explained that he was "able to stay away from alcohol because of his efforts to help other alcoholics."[1] In other words, helping others helped him.

Similarly, breast cancer survivors raise millions of dollars for research. Parents of children with disabilities become fierce advocates for resources. Victims of abuse raise awareness for other victims. Each of these movements emerge from the reality that when you turn your pain into action, especially for others, it heals you.

We know this principle instinctively because it was put in us by God. We were designed by God to heal this way. Not in isolation, but with momentum toward others. In fact, this is the very reason Jesus tells us to "love your neighbor as yourself" (Matt. 22:39). Jesus does not issue this command simply because it is the right thing to do but because it is for our good as well. It draws us out of ourselves. Whenever we welcome a single person into our home, make a meal for a family in crisis, drive a friend's child home from school, check in on someone we haven't heard from in a while, or serve in a ministry that needs us—even when we do so at great personal cost—we are doing what God designed our souls to do.

Jesus's command, then, is not just an instruction for acceptable Christian living. It is much more like a ladder out of a pit. Whether the wound was inflicted yesterday or twenty years ago, the opportunity to love others out of our own pain is always an opportunity to heal it.

REFLECT: What makes it hard for you to reach out to others, especially in seasons of pain? (A few prompts to help you identify why you isolate: shame, fear, vulnerability, or exhaustion.)

Serve Your Neighbor

Hospitality is the ability to pay attention to the guest. This is very difficult, since we are preoccupied with our own needs, worries, and tensions, which prevent us from taking distance from ourselves in order to pay attention to others.

HENRI NOUWEN

Now when it was time for supper, the devil had already put it into the heart of Judas, Simon Iscariot's son, to betray him. Jesus knew that the Father had given everything into his hands, that he had come from God, and that he was going back to God. So he got up from supper, laid aside his outer clothing, took a towel, and tied it around himself. Next, he poured water into a basin and began to wash his disciples' feet and to dry them with the towel tied around him.

John 13:2–5

Sometimes the best way to deny the self, to crucify our vanity, to prune our pride, or to hold accountable our thirst for fame is to intentionally deprive ourselves of these things. When our focus is small and self-oriented, the solution is simple: serve others.

This is one of the last spiritual practices that Jesus models for his disciples before his death. It's a remarkable choice, in view of what Jesus is about to endure. Within twenty-four hours, Jesus will be stripped of all that he has: his dignity, his community, his health, his life. He is facing unimaginable suffering, and yet he does not spend his final hours indulging in the finer things. He does not ask his disciples to pamper him so that he will be physically ready for the day ahead. He does not, once and for all, disclose every remaining detail about who he is and then demand to be treated accordingly.

Instead, in the final moments before he is brought low, Jesus willingly lowers himself first, in service to his students.

Consistent with most of his stories, Jesus is not just modeling a way *of* life but a path *to* life. Service rightly orients our souls off of ourselves and draws us out of ourselves. When pain, anxiety, or insecurity threaten to turn our focus inward, serving others actively resists that gravitational pull.

As his followers, we always have this option when the walls of pain are closing in. As our vision shrinks inward and we are tempted toward self-pity, self-righteousness, isolation, or despair, Jesus's last communal act stands as a soul-nurturing alternative. We can participate in pulling our focus outward through service.

But that is not all. Jesus did not simply serve his disciples; he lowered himself in the process. He practiced a *humble* sort of service, not a posturing that subtly made him into a martyr. This humbling is important, because insecurity has a paradoxical effect on the soul: It shrivels our focus, while enticing us to puff ourselves up. For many of us, we cope with our feelings of loneliness, rejection, or hiddenness by centering ourselves even more. We post more frequently on social media, we bend conversations to focus back on us, or we even serve others conspicuously, in order to be noticed.

The effect of this centering is that we diminish ourselves spiritually as we try to enlarge ourselves externally. This is the temptation of pain, especially that of insecurity.

It is also a temptation that Jesus knew. Hebrews 4:15 tells us that Jesus was tempted "in every way." Although he never sinned, we can surmise from this verse that Jesus knew the allure of putting himself and his comfort first. Rather than cave to this temptation, he "crucified" it by actively lowering himself at a moment when he very well may have desired the opposite.

If you find yourself in that place today—feeling alone, left out, overlooked, or unseen—Jesus has so much compassion for you. No one understands better than he does. That is why he entered into our pain to show us the way out. As the Spirit leads, consider how you might pry your focus off of your self and raise your gaze through serving others. This may look like folding your kids' laundry with a generous heart, giving anonymously to a person in need, reaching out to an elderly person in your neighborhood or community and simply listening to them, or volunteering at your church in a role that you might not prefer but know is needed. Regardless of what you choose, do it with humility, and for the glory of God. This is not only the Christian way of life but the path *to* life.

REFLECT: Take some time to ask the Holy Spirit how you might practice humble service in your life. Be honest with him and with yourself about what would be most soul purifying for you, in the best and most life-giving ways.

Pray for Your Neighbor

Prayer is like waking up from a nightmare to reality. We laugh at what we took so seriously inside the dream. We realize that all is truly well. . . . Prayer brings perspective, shows the big picture, gets you out of the weeds, reorients you to where you really are.

TIM KELLER

I give thanks to my God for every remembrance of you, always praying with joy for all of you in my every prayer, because of your partnership in the gospel from the first day until now. I am sure of this, that he who started a good work in you will carry it on to completion until the day of Christ Jesus.

Philippians 1:3–6

In 2021, actor and *Star Trek* legend William Shatner made history by journeying to space in a privately owned capsule called *The New Shepard*. This accomplishment was

185

the fulfillment of a lifelong dream, and yet his reaction was not at all what he anticipated. Rather than cause him to laugh or cheer in delight, the sight of the earth from space elicited grief: "It was the death that I saw in space and the lifeforce that I saw coming from the planet—the blue, the beige and the white," he said. "And I realized one was death and the other was life. . . . I wept for the Earth because I realized it's dying."[1]

Shatner was not prepared for his response, but it was not a unique one. His experience is so common, in fact, that it has a name: the overview effect. The term was first coined in 1987 by "space philosopher" Frank White, who defined it as "a cognitive and emotional shift in a person's awareness, their consciousness and their identity when they see the Earth from space."[2] As a result of this shift, astronauts describe feeling intense emotions such as appreciation for the earth, concern for the fragility of the world, and—in the absence of visible borders—a deeper connection to humanity on the whole.

Although only a handful of people in the history of the world have been able to experience the overview effect from space, there is a real sense in which we experience the same zoomed-out, big-picture vision whenever we pray, especially when we pray for others. As we go throughout our days focusing on whatever is directly in front of us—our desires, our worries, our cares—our sense of the world grows smaller and smaller, while our sense of ourselves grows larger.

Thankfully, prayer is always available to raise our gaze. When we pray to God about others, we are not only moving our hearts into alignment with his but drawing our vision outward. It is the simplest, most accessible way to unbend the soul.

To put it another way, prayer restores us to reality. Through prayer, our struggles are rightsized in proportion to the pain of others. Our sense of self is returned to its proper dimensions. And we are wrested out of our own soul-spiraling isolation with the reminder that others are hurting too.

This is the gentle power of intercessory prayer. It allows us to focus on others without diminishing ourselves. Instead, it simply invites us to shift our perspective.

REFLECT: If you do not already have one, start a short list of people you would like to pray for more regularly. Consider putting this list on your mirror or in your phone, and whenever you pray for them, pay close attention to what God is shifting in you.

Heal for Your Neighbor

All great spirituality is about what we do with our pain. If we do not transform our pain, we will transmit it to those around us.

RICHARD ROHR

Therefore, since we have been justified by faith, we have peace with God through our Lord Jesus Christ. We have also obtained access through him by faith into this grace in which we stand, and we boast in the hope of the glory of God. And not only that, but we also boast in our afflictions, because we know that affliction produces endurance, endurance produces proven character, and proven character produces hope. This hope will not disappoint us, because God's love has been poured out in our hearts through the Holy Spirit who was given to us.

Romans 5:1–5

One of the most paralyzing lies of insecurity is that it is meaningless. When we aren't invited to a party, or we go through a breakup, or we don't get the promotion, or we suffer some relatively minor rejection or humiliation, it's tempting to believe these aches are superficial and therefore below the attention of God. "God has bigger problems to solve," we assume. "This personal embarrassment, or minor setback, is not important enough to bring to the cross."

So we try to handle it ourselves.

Whenever we do this—whenever we choose not to involve God—we forfeit an opportunity to experience comfort, hope, and healing in any measure. We also forfeit the possibility of *purpose*, because God can only redeem the pain that we bring to him.

The truth is that no pain—no matter how seemingly insignificant or small—lies outside the bounds of God's redemption. There is nothing in all of creation that has been touched by sin that will not be restored by God. Nothing. And that includes our silliest or most insignificant wounds. No matter the size of the heartache or the severity of the sting, God will wipe away every tear. Every single one. And then, once our tears have dried, he will lift our gaze upward to notice those around us who are hurting similarly, who we might not have ever noticed otherwise.

But he won't stop there. Because God is generous and extravagant, he is interested not in simply healing our pain but in redeeming it for the healing of others. Profound purpose can emerge from our pain, but we will fail to recognize it if we wallow in our insecurity or assume it is too small a thing for God.

That is why these lesser wounds often do seem meaningless—because we allow them to be. In fact, it is sometimes the smaller injuries that take longer to heal, precisely because we do not think to bring them to Jesus. We are less likely to make this mistake with great and serious suffering, because our hands are somewhat forced. In moments of debilitating pain, we are well aware of our human limitations and our desperate need for God to sustain us. It is the ordinary bumps that we try to muddle through on our own.

The invitation—and the challenge—of these common, everyday struggles is not to experience them in vain. It is entirely possible to endure hardship and to learn nothing from it, to grow no closer to God, to injure others with our unhealed wounds, and to make our souls smaller as a result. This is true of trials both big and small: Our pain can be in vain.

But it doesn't have to be.

Ever since Jesus turned a symbol of torture into a symbol of hope, no broken thing has been beyond the redemption of God—or below it. From the splinters to the beams, the cross is a down payment on what God can do with your pain. Your hurt feelings, your bruised ego, your small indignities—even these can become birthplaces of redemption.

And the world will be better for it.

REFLECT: What "lesser" pain, or insecurity, are you experiencing right now, and what might God be teaching you through it? Remember, God does not cause suffering or loss in order to teach us something, but he can nevertheless redeem it. What are some redemptive possibilities for these smaller aches?

Looking at God Looking at You

We all are born into the world looking for someone look-ing for us.

CURT THOMPSON

The LORD looks down from heaven;
he observes everyone.
He gazes on all the inhabitants of the earth
from his dwelling place.
He forms the hearts of them all;
he considers all their works. . . .

May your faithful love rest on us, LORD,
for we put our hope in you.

Psalm 33:13–15, 22

P rolonged eye contact is a surprisingly intimate gesture, which is why it can feel awkward or even aggressive. I am always keenly aware when I am speaking to someone who engages in intense eye contact. On the one hand, I do not want the people I'm talking to, to be distracted on their phone or staring across the room. I *do* want them engaged in what I am saying. But if they swing too far in the opposite direction—staring into the depths of my soul while I'm merely describing the restaurant I tried last Friday—it's too much. I will intentionally break eye contact, sometimes by looking at the ground or in the air, just to grant myself some social space.

Of course, there is one notable exception to this social norm, which is the context of romance. When a young couple is falling in love, extended eye contact is not only appropriate but also blissful. When you gaze into another person's eyes, and they gaze back, it is not simply a form of connection but a form of delight. You are present, engaged, and captivated.

This is, in many ways, the type of gazing that God invites us into. He does not invite us to look upon him in reverence while his head is turned elsewhere. He is not distracted by all that is going on in the world, like a parent tethered to his phone while his child fights to compel his attention. Nor is God so far off that we are staring into an anonymous sky, occupied by a faceless, distant Father.

No, we gaze upon a God who gazes back.

In fact, anytime we meditate on God's Word, number his attributes, contemplate his character, or remember his deeds, we are not initiating this gesture of intimacy, because God never stopped. He never ceases to gaze on us with affection and love. It is we who simply forget.

This is the sweetness of self-forgetfulness. God invites us to lift our gaze so that we will discover we are already seen, considered, and prioritized by the One who is infinitely more powerful and loving than ourselves.

The life of faith is, in many ways, one of mutual adoration. We love in response to God's love. We delight in response to God's delight. This is why, for centuries, Christians have read the Song of Solomon as an allegory for God's love. We who look upon Jesus are locked in a lover's gaze.

As you continue the journey of self-forgetfulness, of reorienting your soul off of self and back onto God—a journey you will embark on again and again throughout your life—do it not out of guilt or shame or obligation. Do it with this knowledge:

You are seen.

You are known.

You are considered.

You are cherished.

You are pursued.

You are loved.

Before any one of us ever lifts our eyes off of self and onto our Father in heaven, we must remember, he is the God who gazes at us.

REFLECT: Imagine Jesus standing next to you this very moment. What is the expression on his face? How does he look at you? What is in his eyes? What does he want you to know, or to feel, today?

ACKNOWLEDGMENTS

As I think back on the inspiration for this devotional, the first thank-you that leaps to mind is to my publisher, Baker Books, for supporting me in this project. Because this is a revisiting of ideas and themes from my first book, *Free of Me*, which Baker had already published and championed, they did not have to put more resources behind it, but I am so grateful that they did. Baker has believed in me, my writing, and my books from the get-go, and I am so thankful to be a part of the Baker family.

On that note, I also want to thank my editors Stephanie Smith and Robin Turici. Stephanie is a best-in-class editor whose feedback I trust implicitly. She is encouraging, thorough, honest, and brilliant. Robin, likewise, is an author's dream. She is meticulous, theologically exacting (in the best way), and just so smart. My writing is only bettered by their collective wisdom and skill.

I am also grateful for my agent, Alex Field, who believed in this project and supported me from the jump. From the day I sent him a random email floating the idea for this devotional, he ran with it and advocated for it all along the way.

As always, I owe an unpayable debt to my parents, without whom I could not do half the things I do. They are not only my biggest cheerleaders but also the village that helps us raise our kids. Even when I have a deadline and my workload is overwhelming, my kids are thoroughly seen, cared for, and spoiled by my parents' devoted attention to them.

And most of all, thank you to Ike, who truly makes all of this possible. I write, speak, and lead in our church because he believes that I should, and he puts his money where his mouth is. When I am writing or preparing a message, he clears away as much space as I need to do it. He does this selflessly and joyfully, and I am just ridiculously grateful that this wonderful man is my husband. I love you, Ike!

NOTES

Before You Begin

1. Alison Cook, *The Best of You: Break Free from Painful Patterns, Mend Your Past, and Discover Your True Self in God* (Thomas Nelson, 2023), 11.
2. Tim Keller, *The Freedom of Self-Forgetfulness: The Path to True Christian Joy* (10Publishing, 2012), 32.

Day 2 Notice Your Scripts

1. S. K. Fineberg et al., "Self-Reference in Psychosis and Depression: A Language Marker of Illness," *Psychological Medicine* 46, no. 12 (2016): 2605–15, https://pubmed.ncbi.nlm.nih.gov/27353541/.

Day 3 Notice Your Assumptions

1. Brené Brown, "Clear Is Kind. Unclear Is Unkind," Brené Brown, October 15, 2018, https://brenebrown.com/articles/2018/10/15/clear-is-kind-unclear-is-unkind/.

Day 5 Notice Your Narcissism

1. As quoted in Chuck DeGroat, "When Narcissism Comes to . . . Church Doctrine (Part I - Introduction)," *Chuck DeGroat* (blog), accessed July 9, 2024, https://www.chuckdegroat.net/chuck-degroat-blog/2018/07/08/when-narcissism-comes-to-church-doctrine-part-1-introduction.

Day 9 The Elusive True Self

1. Tim Keller (@TimKellerNYC), "So Christian identity is received, not achieved," X, April 12, 2021, 9:32 a.m., https://x.com/timkellernyc/status/1381601155877322754?s=20.
2. C. S. Lewis, *Mere Christianity* (HarperCollins, 2001), 225.

Day 16 What It Means to Deny the Self

1. Cook, *The Best of You*, 11.

Day 20 Receiving Exclusion

1. C. S. Lewis, "The Inner Ring," in *The Weight of Glory* (HarperCollins, 2001), 146.

Day 21 Receiving Loneliness

1. Henri Nouwen, *The Wounded Healer: Ministry in Contemporary Society* (Image Double Day, 1979), 90.

Day 22 Receiving Hiddenness

1. Dallas Willard, *The Spirit of the Disciplines: Understanding How God Changes Lives* (HarperOne, 1999), 172–73 (italics added).

Day 24 Receiving Insignificance

1. Jen Wilkin, *Women of the Word: How to Study the Bible with Both Our Hearts and Our Minds* (Crossway, 2019), 23–24.

Day 35 Look for Laughter

1. Mayo Clinic Staff, "Stress Relief from Laughter? It's No Joke," Mayo Clinic, September 22, 2023, https://www.mayoclinic.org/healthy-lifestyle/stress-management/in-depth/stress-relief/art-20044456.
2. Steve Cuss, *Managing Leadership Anxiety: Yours and Theirs* (Thomas Nelson, 2019), 117.
3. Cuss, *Managing Leadership Anxiety*, 143.
4. As quoted in Mari-Anna Stålnacke, "Laughter and Good Cheer," Flowing Faith, May 27, 2016, https://flowingfaith.com/2016/05/laughter-and-good-cheer.html.

Day 36 Love Your Neighbor

1. Francis Hartigan, *Bill W.: A Biography of Alcoholics Anonymous Co-founder Bill Wilson* (Thomas Dunne Books, 2000), 85.

Day 38 Pray for Your Neighbor

1. Enrique Rivera, "William Shatner Experienced Profound Grief in Space. It Was the 'Overview Effect,'" NPR, October 23, 2022, https://www.npr.org/2022/10/23/1130482740/william-shatner-jeff-bezos-space-travel-overview-effect.

2. Rivera, "William Shatner."

ABOUT *the* AUTHOR

SHARON HODDE MILLER, PhD, is teaching pastor at Bright City Church in Durham, North Carolina, which she cofounded with her husband, Ike. The author of *Free of Me*, *Nice*, and *The Cost of Control*, Miller has blogged at SheWorships.com for over ten years; has been a regular contributor to Propel, Her.meneutics, and She Reads Truth; and has  written for *Relevant*, *Christianity Today*, (in)courage, and many other publications and blogs. She lives with Ike and their three children in Durham, North Carolina.

CONNECT WITH SHARON

SharonHoddeMiller.com

@SharonHoddeMiller

@SharonHMiller

@SHoddeMiller